PRAISE FOR
EVERY DAY, I'M BRAVE

"In sharing her deeply personal battle with anxiety, Renee Zukin provides a testament to human resilience. *Every Day, I'm Brave* is a beautiful reminder that bravery is a daily choice—a journey that leads to a life of endless possibility and fulfillment."

–Marci Shimoff, *New York Times* best-selling author of
Happy for No Reason and *Chicken Soup for the Woman's Soul*

"Renee Zukin's *Every Day, I'm Brave* is a vulnerable and inspiring perspective from someone in the trenches with OCD. With mental health conditions on the rise, it is inspiring to read the account of someone who has figured out how to transform their challenges into growth and transformation, teaching all of us that fear does not need to define us. A courageous book all around!"

–Betsy Rippentrop, PhD, licensed psychologist,
Dr. Yoga Momma; author of *Chakra Healing:
Renew Your Life Force with the Chakras' Seven Energy Centers*

"Renee Zukin's inspirational account of her journey through anxiety and fear offers readers a manual for living with courage. With compassionate storytelling and practical guidance, this book offers hope for those seeking to live authentically amidst life's uncertainties."

–Sage Lavine, author and CEO, Women Rocking Business

"A powerful narrative of transformation, Renee Zukin's *Every Day, I'm Brave* offers readers the tools necessary to traverse their own landscapes of fear. Her blend of personal experience and actionable advice fosters a deep sense of hope and agency."

–Jena Schwartz, poet, essayist, writing coach, and author of *Fierce
Encouragement: 201 Writing Prompts for Staying Grounded in Fragile Times*

"*Every Day, I'm Brave* is an essential read for anyone who experiences anxiety and self-doubt so that they, too, can feel empowered and hopeful that change is possible."

–Pamela Slim, award-winning author of *The Widest Net: Unlock Untapped Markets and Discover New Customers Right in Front of You*; speaker; cofounder, K'é Community Lab

"*Every Day, I'm Brave* is more than a book; it's an invitation to go on a liberating journey from fear to self-empowerment. Run, don't walk, to get your copy."

–Julie Steelman, feminine business mentor, The Prosperous Feminine; award-winning wildlife photographer

"*Every Day, I'm Brave* takes readers on a journey to discover how to move from immobilizing fear to letting courage lead."

–Keith Leon S., award-winning international best-selling author, book publisher, and filmmaker

"Renee Zukin masterfully weaves a journey of resilience, self-acceptance, and transformation. Through her deeply personal reflections, she invites us to shift from unconscious vulnerability to courageous presence, reminding us that bravery is not about fearlessness but about choosing to show up anyway."

–Dev Suroop Kaur, founder, Empowered Voice; mentor in vocal confidence and expression

"Renee Zukin writes a compassion-driven story about how she gained courage to face paralyzing fears and ultimately transform her life. *Every Day, I'm Brave* is a must-read for anyone who seeks inspiration to reach for their dreams despite anxiety and self-doubt."

–Beverly Blasingame, writer and entrepreneur

"Renee's brave account shows how vulnerability can be our greatest strength and help us overcome even the most difficult obstacles. Her story is a profile in hope and self-compassion, with so many rich lessons."

–Kate Moreland, JD, empowerment coach,
Kate Moreland Coaching & Consulting

"This book is a must-read for anyone anywhere who has ever been afraid of things they cannot control. Renee Zukin created a gift in the form of her memoir as she shares her courageous journey through the shadows of OCD toward a life defined by hope and resilience. With unflinching honesty and warmth, Renee transforms her personal battle into a universal call for strength, showing that bravery is not the absence of fear but the decision to keep moving forward. Her story is a luminous reminder that every day holds the promise of a new beginning, inspiring anyone who's ever doubted their power to reclaim it and embrace change."

–Athena Llewellyn, founder and creatrix, Brand Aura;
cofounder, SPASHIP

"*Every Day, I'm Brave* is a testament that the impossible is indeed possible with encouragement, strength, and love. Make sure you have tissues and a journal handy when reading Renee's story. The Brave Reflection sections listed in each chapter give you a front row seat to do the work for yourself that Renee has been doing for decades. If you are ready to have your soul opened and your mind calmed, pick up her guide to life today."

–Kellee Forkenbrock, author; public services librarian, North Liberty
Library; owner, Goddess Grounded

"Renee Zukin fearlessly exposes places in herself that many of us would not want to share with anyone, much less with everyone! Her words made me feel less alone and reminded me of the wisdom of the poet Hafiz: 'Fear is the cheapest room in the house. I would like to see you living in better conditions.' I hope you'll read this compassionate book if your fears are keeping you small."

—Jennifer New, author; founder, Hypha

"*Every Day, I'm Brave* is an invitation to rewrite the stories fear tells us. With honesty and heart, Renee Zukin offers a powerful blend of personal insight and practical guidance, showing us how to turn life's challenges into stepping stones for growth."

—Megan Walrod, founder and women's empowerment coach,
Live Your Yes; author of *It's Always Been Me*

EVERY DAY, I'M BRAVE

EVERY DAY, I'M BRAVE

Cultivating Resilience *to* Gain Freedom *from* Fear

RENEE ZUKIN

WONDERWELL
PRESS

Published by Wonderwell Press
Austin, Texas
www.gbgpress.com

This work is being published under the Wonderwell Press imprint by an exclusive arrangement with Wonderwell. Wonderwell, Wonderwell Press, and the Wonderwell logos are wholly-owned trademarks of Wonderwell.

Distributed by Greenleaf Book Group

For ordering information or special discounts for bulk purchases, please contact Greenleaf Book Group at PO Box 91869, Austin, TX 78709, 512.891.6100.

Design and composition by Greenleaf Book Group and Sheila Parr
Cover design by Greenleaf Book Group and Sheila Parr
Cover image used under license from Adobe Stock: 1030541076/ARTIFICIAN

Publisher's Cataloging-in-Publication data is available.

Print ISBN: 978-1-963827-25-5

eBook ISBN: 978-1-963827-26-2

To offset the number of trees consumed in the printing of our books, Greenleaf donates a portion of the proceeds from each printing to the Arbor Day Foundation. Greenleaf Book Group has replaced over 50,000 trees since 2007.

Printed in the United States of America on acid-free paper

25 26 27 28 29 30 31 32   10 9 8 7 6 5 4 3 2 1

First Edition

For you, with love.

CONTENTS

WATCHING JETS
ON A SUNDAY AFTERNOON
2010

One of these days I will just decide to be unafraid.

I will buy a ticket, shake hands with the pilot,

And find a window seat in row 10.

And it will go like that: in a quiet resolve.

The heat no longer brazen in my chest;

The scattered and hurried thoughts, absent.

In its place will be a comfort,

A knowledge that I beat the fear of death

And conquered every bit of darkness

That creeps under my skin. I will be only Light.

And Light will take me anywhere I wish to go.

INTRODUCTION

ONE MORNING, AFTER DROPPING MY fiancé, Andrew, off at the airport and running late for work, I began internally grumbling as I drove. I kept thinking about how so many people would tell Andrew how brave he was to do the educational work he did in developing countries. Just the night before, as we chatted with other parents during intermission at my eldest daughter's school play, he was retelling a story about alleviating the tension during an armed raid of his office in South Sudan.

"Wow, weren't you scared?" our friend asked, leaning in closer to hear him.

"Definitely, but I had a feeling we'd be okay," Andrew noted, going into more detail about the lollipops he'd handed out that put smiles on the guards' faces. "They ended up taking all our computers; then, the embassy folks took us all across the border, where we got to stay on a beach resort for like a week."

"You're so brave to do that kind of work."

Alone in my car, I sighed at the conversation. Andrew was often traveling to remote areas, some of them riddled with violence, so it's true that it took great courage to do those things. However, being the one left stateside to work the consistent corporate education job and look after the house and kids muddled that perspective for me. It's not that I couldn't have traveled with him now and then; it's that I *wouldn't*. I was too afraid to fly, too afraid to be in environments where I couldn't control what I was eating or how I was getting from place to place. I felt that I couldn't leave my kids because I'd be paralyzed by catastrophic thoughts and separation anxiety—and left defenseless and alone with that darkness.

More and more, I had become resentful toward Andrew, and I was angry that those of us who struggle daily with anxiety or depression, who are bogged down with stress, confusion, and responsibilities that demand our full attention, don't receive the same kind of accolades in small talk at parties or the big awards that people like Andrew often receive at banquets.

When I finally got to the office building, I headed to the break room first to wash my hands before taking my breakfast to my cubicle. As I pumped soap into my palm, the internal monologue got louder and more potent.

You know what? It's fucking brave that I got out of bed today. It's fucking brave that I am about to even eat this breakfast despite being afraid of what might be in it. And it's brave that I got my kids to school on time despite the morning chaos.

I diligently scrubbed in between my knuckles and pumped the soap dispenser again for a second round of washing.

It's also brave that I continue to show up here in this soul-sucking job day after day because I'm responsible and I prioritize my kids, making sure this family runs well enough and keeping a roof over our heads.

My left hand swirled suds deep into the crevices of my right palm and then moved to the fingertips.

It's brave that despite the swirling fear in my head and the panic that ensues without notice on a regular basis, I continue to show up in my life every day.

Switching hands, I paid close attention underneath my fingernails before rinsing the soap a final time.

You know what? I paused and felt the warm water spilling out of my hands into the sink. *I am fucking brave. I don't need to ride in airplanes, or travel the world, or walk a tightrope, or feed a shark to be brave. I am brave . . . Every. Single. Day.*

I took a deep breath and walked out of the room toward my cubicle, standing a little taller than before. This wasn't the first pep talk I'd given myself, but it was certainly different. This idea that I could be proud of the little things I did to make my way through the anxiety that I faced regularly would help me forge a path toward transforming my relationship with fear in the years ahead.

Now, more than ever, as we move through the aftermath of a global pandemic, people of all ages are experiencing anxiety in record numbers. According to the National Alliance on Mental Illness, one in five US adults experience mental illness each year.[1] Not only are there many suffering globally, but a recent study from the Association of American Medical Colleges found that "access to care and treatment for mental health issues remains out of reach for most of the population in the United States."[2] With a taxed and challenging health-care system, we have to look for avenues of support and healing that are more accessible and holistic. Moreover, we have to be willing to have the difficult and vulnerable conversations about what it is like to move through life when fear holds us back.

It wasn't until my early thirties that I was accurately diagnosed with obsessive-compulsive disorder (OCD) and, more than a decade later, panic disorder and agoraphobia. Anxiety and depression plagued me in cycles throughout my teenage years and early adulthood, but those, too, I understand much differently now in the context of OCD.

For me, the OCD diagnosis wasn't a dead end or nail in the coffin of hope; it was a beautiful beginning. I was able to see my thoughts, behaviors, habits, and beliefs from a whole new perspective. Not only that, but together with my cognitive behavioral therapy (CBT) practitioners, I was better able to understand and *use* the tools and strategies that would work more effectively with my certain brand of brain. I don't allow the labels to

---

1   "Mental Health by the Numbers," National Alliance on Mental Illness, updated April 2023, https://www.nami.org/about-mental-illness/mental-health-by-the-numbers.

2   Hemangi Modi, Kendal Orgera, and Atul Grover, "Exploring Barriers to Mental Health Care in the US" (issue brief), Association of American Medical Colleges Research and Action Institute, October 10, 2022, https://www.aamcresearchinstitute.org/our-work/issue-brief/exploring-barriers -mental-health-care-us.

define who I am, but they do help provide insight into what works and what doesn't and why. For that, I am ever grateful.

I also dove deep into the teachings of visionaries, mystics, scientists, and researchers such as Gary Zukov, Katie and Gay Hendricks, Mel Robbins, and Brené Brown. However, as I explored what it meant to live consciously and understood more fully the belief I'd always had that G-d, Universe, Source lives at the apex of science and spirituality, I kept bumping up against what was supposed to be a simple and profound way to move throughout the world: *Trust your inner guidance.*

How was I going to be able to "trust my gut" or "hear the still, small voice" when anxiety and panic had such loud voices making the inner compass difficult to discern? The years of habituated thought patterns and instant physiological responses created lies that were difficult to ignore. "Trust your gut" was great advice—unless your gut was feeding you total misinformation. How would I begin to not only hear and connect to my inner wisdom but also to heed its instructions when every fiber of my ego, my being, was telling me to resist, avoid, run, and hide? This would become the most complex and meaningful work ahead.

What I have come to understand while working to manage anxiety, panic, and OCD symptoms is that we have to create new ways of interacting with any diagnosis to feel better, to work better, and to engage with the world better. Understanding what those new ways are for each of us individually takes trial and error. I have read and studied different approaches and research on neuroplasticity, mindfulness, conscious living, energy work, and CBT to figure out what works for me. It is my hope that the legwork I've done can offer you a unique look at the experience and hope for a brighter future forward for you as well.

Let me be clear: I am not a therapist. I am not certified in any psychological modality, and I'm not giving out medical advice here. However, I have spent my life focused on learning more about psychology, behavior change, and self-improvement models. Through the process of earning my master's degree in secondary education, I studied educational and developmental psychology. As a teacher, I stayed on top of new research and methods of behavioral sciences; discipline; emotional intelligence; and cultural awareness, identity, and value systems to be the best instructor, mentor, and caregiver for my students and eventually my clients as well.

I believe that doing the inner work is what creates outer change, and this has been the foundation of my own healing journey. Showing up in service to others often gives me the strength to move through my hardest days. And when I show up better for myself, it allows others to do the same.

The time I've spent in different therapists' offices over decades has allowed me to translate all this knowledge and information into specific steps and perspectives to live my life as best as I can. Perhaps it can be helpful for you to see this distillation—to see, in the context of the narrative, how I've put the things I've learned into practice and how intuition, wisdom, making a lot of mistakes, and learning from them have helped me fill my toolbox. I'm sure you've already got some good tools in your toolbox. But maybe you'll pick up a few more here or see a new and different way to use the ones you've got. Maybe you'll see yourself mirrored in these pages. Or maybe this story will remind you of someone you care about. Whichever the case, my wish is for you to take what is helpful and leave the rest.

The solution to overcoming a mental health diagnosis in order to live a full, heart-centered, and purposeful life is multifaceted. There isn't one magic pill or singular spiritual practice that can "cure" anxiety. In a culture that loves an overnight success story, how do we uplift the stories of ongoing triumph that rely not on a miracle system but a holistic, ongoing approach to sustainable, joyful living? How can we, instead, celebrate all the ways in which we show up bravely every day?

It took a long time for me to write this book. One of the things that often held me back from writing was the fear of placing blame or shedding light on other people's (or my own) seemingly bad behavior, actions, or mistakes. The fear was twofold. First, it could karmically come back to bite me in the ass if I say not-nice things about other people (but I remind myself that this is not my intention). The second fear is that my own mistakes, faults, and challenges will be brought to light and people will judge me harshly for them (no more harshly than I'm sure I've spent years judging myself).

But I came to realize that I am not a victim here in any way, and I hope that perspective rings true throughout this telling. My intention is to illustrate the experience of how fear affected my life, my relationships, and my learning from a personal perspective and not as some Truth with a capital *T*.

So I want to make one thing crystal clear before we dive in: There are no villains in my story; instead, I like to think of them as "challengers"—people I've made agreements with on a soul or cellular level to highlight my path and purpose, with mirrors, lights, and obstacles that show me the way. From a universal, neutral perspective of why we are here, we can see how much, like the cells in the body, we humans are parts of a larger whole, a system that works to create a state of aliveness. So it must be true, then, that each of us play a part.

I honor, respect, and even love the challengers in my life. Although some of these situations and experiences created fear and unpleasantness, they were also the catalyst for me not only to understand myself and my place in this world but also to have compassion and set boundaries for those who challenge me along the way. And for that, I'm grateful.

Rather than writing about being a victim of circumstance or diagnosis, I wanted to write a book about surviving and thriving. This is not so much a book about fear as it is about hope and bravery. It's the story of how I cultivated resilience and created a multifaceted toolbox to help me navigate life's challenges.

That moment in the office break room changed my trajectory. Acknowledging my own courage allowed me to understand that bravery is a spectrum and that one type of brave act isn't more worthy than another. Seeing fear and courage through a more compassionate lens would become the catalyst to embracing the daily challenges of anxiety and OCD differently, allowing me to overcome many of the obstacles I had built up around me over the years. "Every Day, I'm Brave" became a mantra, a celebration, and a reflection that acknowledged what it takes to evolve from being stuck and allowing fear to call the shots to embracing its existence and letting courage lead.

This is the story of that shift.

1

FOOD FIGHT

I HAD BAKED CHICKEN IN THE OVEN AGAIN. It was one of the few times when I actually cooked a full meal for the family: potatoes, salad, and this chicken breast doused in margarine, a little salt and pepper, and some paprika.

It was the fall of 2006, the time of year when you just start to notice it getting darker earlier. My two older kids were sitting down at the table while the baby bounced in her seat next to them on the floor. I stood at the kitchen counter, having successfully cut through each piece of chicken to make sure it was thoroughly cooked. I'd been afraid of *salmonella* lurking in my kitchen for a good couple of months, and tonight would be the last time I'd have to worry about it invading my insides from undercooked chicken.

I plated and served the kids and their dad first before joining them. I sat poised, with my utensils in hand, ritually taking a couple of deep breaths to prepare myself for the experience of eating. I had no appetite. I ate for show most of the time, and I ate because I knew I needed something to sustain me. But I didn't *want* to eat. I didn't want anything except the gnawing pain in my gut to go away or for the lump lodged in my throat each time I swallowed my pride to dissolve. My voice—drowned out by the tension in the house—was often silenced by fear.

I picked up a piece of chicken off my plate with a fork and held it close to my eyes—peering into the meat for hues of pink, turning it this way and that. Unsatisfied that I could trust my sight, I put it down, sliced it smaller still, and lifted it again—only to question whether the coloration was from the last bit of sunlight coming through the window or indeed the sign of uncooked chicken. I put my fork down again and used it to gently scoot the chicken pieces to the side of my plate, creating space between it and the potato I would take a few bites of.

Nick, my husband at the time, looked over at me. "What, now you're not going to eat it?" he said. The judgment in his voice was heavy.

"I don't know," I answered. "I can't tell if it's done."

Nick reached his fork across the table to my plate, stabbed a bite-size piece, and ate it. "It's done," he declared.

I looked down at my plate and took another deep breath, still unconvinced.

By this point, the kids had finished their meals and asked to be excused. I got up and started clearing their plates, leaving my own full plate for last. Nick headed to the front room to catch the end of a football game while the kids played, and the noise drowned out the sounds of me scraping the remnants of my dinner into the trash can. *I'm done*, I thought, as I stared into the mess of scraps before me. It would be at least three years until I dared to eat chicken again, and fear would continue to hold me back in myriad ways.

I had spent so much of my life being afraid—afraid of making people angry, afraid for my and my children's safety, afraid of not having enough money. I was afraid of traveling—by car, by plane, by boat. I was afraid that I'd get sick, get hurt, or die. I was essentially afraid of anything out of my control. These were the big worries that often infiltrated my young mind but didn't much get in the way of my day-to-day life.

As I got older, however, these big fears started to create the foundation on which I would weigh all my decisions. In the process of trying to gain some semblance of control over the anxiety I was feeling more acutely, I slid into a deeply grooved pattern of thought about contamination just a few months after my third child was born.

It was slow and harmless at first. As a family, between my teaching at the middle school, the eldest in elementary, and the two youngest in day care, we had taken turns picking up every virus that traveled through Iowa that year. I was getting so tired of laundering sheets filled with vomit and stuffing my newborn with antibiotics that I became hypervigilant about where illnesses might lurk.

Around the same time, there were spikes in the number of food poisoning cases around the country. *Salmonella* and *E. coli* were showing up in peanut butter, spinach, and dairy products. I was beginning to feel sick every time I ate, and I wondered whether I had contracted some sort of awful intestinal worm.

As a result, I had started washing my hands with more fervor and repetition, as well as using hand sanitizer in my classroom at school (long before it became standard practice). I started shying away from potlucks, questioning who had touched the food, where it came from, or how long it had been sitting out. By the time the summer of 2007 rolled around, I had dropped fifteen good pounds of baby weight just because I stopped eating all the cookies and candies that sat in the staff lunchroom, not because I was disciplined but because I was afraid of the germs that might have infiltrated them.

Being the most common source of *E. coli* and *salmonella*, meat was the next to go from my diet. After months of inspecting every piece of meat to make sure it was completely cooked before I put it in my mouth, I simply crossed it off my list of acceptable foods to eat. I'd already stopped eating beef because of the lingering effects of gallbladder removal surgery, and now poultry, pork, eggs, and fish were a no-go. I didn't have to worry about what was in it if I wasn't going to be eating it. It was just simpler that way.

In addition to a list of foods I would no longer eat, there were other rules to try to ensure that my relative state of good health would remain constant. I required myself to sanitize my hands after handling money, after touching doorknobs, after using the phone, and after shaking hands. I used toilet paper to lock the bathroom stall door of a public restroom and my pinkie fingers to handle cupboards and drawers to keep the surface area of potential contamination of my hands to a minimum. If someone coughed or sneezed while walking down the street toward me, I would hold my breath as I moved through the space in which they had just walked.

However, most heartbreaking of all was that I stopped kissing my children. I would hold them and hug them close, but I could no longer kiss them. Bedtime was the hardest: As I read to them and tucked them in, I would turn my head just enough so their little lips would touch only my cheek. I could not reciprocate. After I turned off the lights, I'd head straight to the bathroom and wash my face, hoping no one would see me wiping love away. The anxiety from potential germs and the risk of getting sick were just too much for me, and I was so utterly ashamed that I would feel this way about my own babies.

Thus, the obsessive thoughts about getting sick and the subsequent compulsive rituals put in place to try to ease the anxiety that took hold were amplified. If I didn't wash my hands, the anxiety would grow steadily into a panic. Observing others around me with the sniffles or mentioning a stomachache was enough to send me to the nearest sink or outside for fresh air. Often, if an intrusive question came into my mind about the safety of whatever was on my plate, it would halt my eating completely.

Looking back, I understand that these were the symptoms of obsessive-compulsive disorder (OCD). What would become even more clear was that underneath the rituals themselves was the heavily distorted thinking that avoiding foods or experiences and the rituals that followed whenever I did encounter something scary would actually keep me safe.

But it would take another few years to reach a diagnosis. I was good at hiding the worst of it, even from myself.

I couldn't really hide much of it from my partner, though, as fear and control leaked its way into every conversation and experience we'd been having. Regardless, even after filing for divorce, Nick and I continued to live together and run as a family unit. It was important to both of us, especially because the kids were so young and neither of us could afford to live on our own. One night, we took the family to Chili's for dinner out, an occasion that became fewer and farther between.

When the server brought our food and everyone was settled, I took a deep breath and placed my knife on the edge of the plate next to the black bean burger.

"I'm so sick of this," I muttered to no one in particular. The kids were happily devouring their meals—the little ones' fingertips dripping with mandarin orange juices.

"Sick of what?" Nick asked, tugging at a tough piece of chicken and eyeing me suspiciously.

My tears were immediate. My heart raced; my thoughts spun—wondering if I'd touched this side or that side of the bun. I worried that the knife I'd just used to cut the black bean burger in half wasn't clean enough. And I was angry with myself for thinking all these thoughts instead of sitting back and enjoying a meal with my family.

"Stop crying," Nick said.

At his command, my oldest daughter looked up, constantly aware of what passed between her father and me. "What's wrong, Mom?" she asked.

"Nothing," I lied. "I'm just so tired of feeling this way."

"So stop," Nick said. And he wasn't wrong, but it's just not that easy.

That's the thing about the human condition: Usually, the remedies are simple, but it takes a more complex process to understand, overcome, and support someone through the work of shifting perspective and being willing and brave enough to try something different. The way we each uniquely need to receive support takes really good, clear communication from all parties involved—something that wasn't always a strong suit between Nick and me.

It is also important to acknowledge the difficulty for the person on the other side, observing all of this angst and self-destruction and feeling powerless to "fix" it. For someone who isn't familiar with experiencing anxiety, who doesn't have obsessive and catastrophic thoughts, or who hasn't learned productive ways to work through moments like these, it can be challenging to know what is best to say or do.

I turned and looked at my daughter, the worry on her face clear. "I'll be fine, Shelby," I reassured her. "Just eat."

And I *was* fine. I let the tears flow for a minute to release the fear and tension out of my system. I took a few more deep breaths and began to eat. Bite by bite, I was conscious of where my hands held the edges of the bun. In the end, my plate was left with an array of bun and black bean edges that I didn't eat; the parts that my fingers had touched were arranged in a scattered circle around my plate.

I wondered, once our divorce was final, whether my eating habits would regain some sense of normalcy. Nick was always adamant that mealtime be special, but we had different definitions of what that looked like. To him, it meant that the kids sat still in their chairs, people took turns talking, and everyone ate their food without a fuss. I came from a different sort of experience, one in which meals consisted of lots of interruptions, giggles, and sometimes even a bit of ruckus. It was a difficult match. I wanted to make him happy; I wanted the kids to be happy. I couldn't make that happen simultaneously, so I'd often shut down or make excuses not to eat together.

Many arguments began at the dinner table, but they certainly didn't end there. In my search for answers about why I was so afraid to eat, I'd read articles online and come up short when everything I typed into WebMD pointed toward an eating disorder. I did learn that anorexia is often tied to feeling out of control, and I wondered whether my fear depended, in part, on the lack of control I felt when trying to keep the peace at the table. I also wondered whether, subconsciously, it was an attention-getter: If my family would focus on my lack of eating, then suddenly they weren't fighting about who poked who with a fork or whose feet needed to be under the table while eating over their plate. The theory was a good one, but it certainly wasn't all-encompassing.

The night I cried at Chili's was a turning point, however. I left the restaurant that night with a sense of urgency about regaining control over the thoughts that plagued me every time I ate. I needed them to weaken or disappear altogether. And for that to happen, I had to learn a little more about trust. I had to trust that what I put in my body was going to nourish it, not hurt it. And it began with that simple thought.

In the months that followed, our marriage counselor became my individual therapist, and she and I did the work to uncover root causes while I looked at ways I could relinquish a little control at home and still feel safe. How could I trust that what was happening in my divorce was going to be okay? How could I trust that Nick would show up in ways I thought we needed? How could I trust that every time I'd eat something, I'd be okay? This was the first step in doing brave work: to be able to acknowledge the uncertainty and trust that what I was putting in my body wouldn't harm me.

About a year later many things had shifted, though the fear that my food was contaminated still loomed large. Nick was officially my ex-husband, and we would continue living together for another year, running the household together from separate bedrooms. However, that too was about to change. It would be challenging for the kids to start splitting time between homes on the weekends, but their resilience would prevail.

One evening after work, Nick walked up to the door of my bedroom holding a Tupperware container full of homemade trail mix, sans raisins, which he could not stand.

"Wanna try some?" he asked and waited. By now, he knew the drill.

"Did you eat any yet?" I asked.

"Nope," he said confidently. "Nobody else's hands have been inside this container." He opened the lid and held it out to me.

I peered inside. "How did you mix it?"

He pulled the container back toward him and replaced the lid. I thought he was going to just walk away, exasperated with the line of questioning. It wouldn't be the first time, and frankly, I didn't blame him. Instead, he shook the container up and down.

"Like this," he laughed as the peanuts, M&Ms, and Reese's Pieces clanked against the sides of the oblong container.

I smiled graciously at his humor. "Oh," I chuckled. "I mean how did you get them in there?" What I really wanted to know was whether he had stuck his hands in the bags of candy to get the contents out.

His answer to my question, of course, was obvious: "I opened the packages and poured them in."

"Did you wash the container first?" I knew my question was absurd, so I curled inside myself, waiting for his sarcasm to smack me in the face.

"Yes," he said quickly. And I immediately doubted him. Why would he wash a perfectly clean container from the cupboard? Only I did that.

"Really?" I looked up at him, surprised. His 6'4" frame towered over me, but his blue eyes expressed no hint that he might be lying.

"Yes," he said again and released a heavy sigh. "I've been waiting for you to get home so I could give you some before I ate it. I know how you are. You and your 'issues.'" He gestured quote marks with only the first two fingers on his left hand because the right still held the trail mix.

"Oh," I said quietly and moved around him to walk the few steps into the kitchen. "Okay, then. But I haven't washed *my* hands yet." I turned the faucet up and to the left, as hot as my hands could handle, and squeezed some dish soap into my palm. I washed quickly because I knew I was just going to grab a bowl for him to dump the trail mix into before I washed my hands again. I turned off the water, grabbed a paper towel, and used the towel to open the cabinet door on my right. I saw that there was only one of *my* bowls left, and I took it down and slid it across the counter.

I only used the big white bowls—the first dishes I ever bought myself. The other bowls in the cabinet were plastic, and the kids used them mostly for cereal in the mornings. We always rinsed them right away after use, but we didn't usually wash the bowls until just before dinner because we were always rushing out the door for work, daycare, and school. Being at the office by 8:30 every morning didn't leave much time for getting three kids ready for school, let alone doing the dishes. And we had never figured out where the dishwasher would go in our tiny house even if we had bought one. But that's not why I didn't use them; in fact, I didn't—and still don't—always wash my own bowls right away either. Rather, in my mind, those plastic bowls were just different. The rules I'd created for doing the dishes, washing, preparing food, and eating didn't generally follow logic. I'd eventually learn how to give myself grace for this.

Nick filled the bowl I gave him and looked at me expectantly. "Thanks," I said, turning back to the sink. This time, I washed my hands a little longer because I knew I was going to be touching the actual food and not just the bowl it was housed in.

When I wash my hands, I don't have a certain number I count to, nor do I sing through multiple renditions of "Row, Row, Row Your Boat" like I've heard other people with OCD might do. But I *am* cognizant of all the places the soap reaches—being certain that the bubbles cover the front and back of my hands, paying special attention to the fingertips and in between my knuckles. I even scrub my wrists, cuffing a wrist with one hand while rotating the other hand back and forth. The friction is what cleans the germs off. I know I read that somewhere, or my mom mentioned it to me in passing. In the absence of soap, rubbing your hands under water works almost as well. Luckily, I almost never run out of soap.

The excessive handwashing is mostly connected to eating and preparing food. A few handshakes here and there might prompt me to discreetly pump some hand sanitizer into my palm, but if I'm not about to eat, I can usually wait it out and flutter my fingertips at my sides to remind myself that they've been touched until I can find a sink.

But that time—standing in my kitchen with my rinsed hands, holding the freshly poured bowl of trail mix—I was calmer than I'd been in months. I took a couple deep breaths and thought about trust. I repeated a few words to help anchor it and keep the obsessive, worried thoughts at bay: *I am healthy. This food is safe to eat.* I held that feeling of trust in my mind and heart while I dumped a handful of the mix into my mouth.

In these situations, once the first bite is down, I can usually eat the rest of a meal or snack without much reservation. *What's done is done*, I sometimes have to say to myself as a way to relieve the anxiety that can run rivers up and down my spine.

That evening in the kitchen, it wasn't that I really thought the candy was going to make me sick, though it certainly wasn't the healthiest thing for me to be eating. It was the fact that someone else—in this case, my ex-husband—had prepared it. I was relearning how to trust someone else. And I was learning how to trust myself to discern what and who I could trust.

Brave Reflection

Learning to trust myself, even when I couldn't be completely certain whether what I was eating was safe or how my loved ones were handling food preparation, was a brave act that I would have to confront daily. In many ways, fear is the opposite of trust. Although you may not be afraid that your food is contaminated, I'm guessing you may have other worries that occupy your mind. Some may be reasonable, some a little far-fetched, but we don't need to judge or compare. What matters is that we not only take some time to reflect on what we are afraid of but also choose how we will show up even when we experience fear.

I invite you to take some time to reflect. Use the following questions to guide you in a journal response. Let the pen or your fingers on the keyboard just keep going (I often like to set a timer to get me started; five or ten minutes is a good place to start), and see what comes up for you.

- How can you choose to trust, even if you don't have certainty or solid evidence of what the outcome of your actions will be?
- How can you rebuild trust within yourself and others, even if people or experiences in the past have made it feel more difficult to do so?
- How can you trust the process when you don't always know the end result?

If you'd like to share your insights on social media, use #EveryDayImBrave so that we can celebrate your bravery and acknowledge that you are not alone in this work. For further resources and support, head over to www.everydayimbrave.com.

2

MASKING

I STAYED FOCUSED ON THE CAR in front of me and gripped the steering wheel tightly, too afraid to shift my posture in case I veered off. My son and I were driving back from Northwestern University, a day of college visits tacked on to a dance competition where he took home first place overall for a group tap number that had quickly become a crowd favorite. We had hit Interstate 88 just as the morning commute began, and Evan quickly drifted off to sleep after reclining the passenger seat as far back as it would go.

The ride started off okay. It was daylight, the sky was overcast, and things looked relatively clear on the weather radar I had repeatedly checked for the four-hour ride home. After about thirty minutes, though, the lines on the road started playing tricks on my eyes as they passed quickly by and more cars entered the eight-lane highway. My heart rate quickened as the tunnel vision began, and I focused on my breathing. Four counts in, seven counts out. The longer I can stretch out the out breath, the slower the beats.

My son snored softly. I didn't want to wake him, but I could feel the panic intensifying with each passing second.

I can do this, I said to myself. *Just stay focused on the road ahead. The cars can pass you. Your job is to just maintain speed and stay in your lane.*

The heat was blazing in my chest; a pressure mounted the back of my neck, making it seem like I was being forced to duck—duck and cover from an imaginary danger.

Just keep your foot on the gas pedal, I thought. *You can't stop in the middle of the road.*

I quickly checked the speedometer: 58.

I willed the ball of my foot to apply a little more pressure on the gas and move the needle to 64, closer to a respectable speed as the cars whizzed past me. My eyes darted quickly back and forth from the speedometer to the bumper ahead of me in the distance, and a falling sensation settled in.

Just keep holding the steering wheel, I told myself.

Tears began to flow; I breathed erratically. I really didn't want to wake my son. I wanted to be the mom who could handle driving her kid to college visits. I wanted to be the mom who was strong enough to overcome her fears. I wanted to be the mom who was the adult, who didn't need to lean on a seventeen-year-old kid to get me through a normal, busy commute.

But I could no longer control my breath, and I began to quietly sob. Tears blurred my vision, and I held on to the steering wheel even tighter.

"What's happening?" I heard Evan's voice echo through the noise in my head. "Why are you crying? What's happening?" He bolted upright and looked around, noting the traffic, my speedometer, and that all was actually well on the outside.

He put his hand on my back, and I breathed into the weight of it.

"It's okay," he reassured me. "Let's get off at the next exit."

"I'm too scared to change lanes," I replied.

"It's okay," he said again. "I'll let you know when it's clear. Just keep your eyes on the road."

He helped navigate us to the nearest off-ramp, and we eased off the interstate. I didn't even make it to the stoplight and instead pulled completely off to the side of the road. When the car finally stopped moving and I shifted into park, I crumbled.

That moment, I knew I had reached my capacity to mask the severity of the ongoing panic and anxiety I'd been holding on to for years. I was unable to keep it together for my kids, barely eating or straying far from home, and by this time, even a simple trip to the grocery store was disorienting and inwardly humiliating. I was working so hard on protecting the projection that everything was okay on the outside that my insides became unmanageable, unbearable. I was defeated, and what I would soon learn was that it wasn't the fear itself that was winning but the shame and guilt trying to cover it all up.

Masking is a term often used in mental health spaces to describe hiding or repressing symptoms to blend in with others around you.[1] Masking has also been referred to as a way to compensate for or repress and hide symptoms often fueled by social pressures or expectations. The mask is a face that we can sometimes put on to hide the fear; to keep up with the Joneses, so to speak; and to make life look okay on the outside when inside, the alarms are blaring.

In some ways, it can be beneficial to mask—a sort of trick of the mind to keep more severe symptoms in check—except that it can be exhausting and lead to more stress, anxiety, and burnout. And, as in the preceding case, masking can sometimes result in more of a pressure-cooker situation: Without being able to acknowledge and allow the feelings of panic to flow and expire, the work it takes to keep it together can actually exacerbate what's happening.

Moreover, a lot of masking is rooted in shame. Do we need to generally behave in ways deemed appropriate by societal and cultural norms at work, at school, and in other social situations? Of course we do. I can't go screaming down the hallway in the middle of a work meeting when I

---

1   Amy Marschall, "Suppressing Emotions or Behaviors? You Might Be 'Masking,'" VeryWell Mind, updated June 7, 2024, https://www.verywellmind.com/what-is-masking-in-mental-health -6944532.

feel my flight-or-fight response suddenly engage. But I *can* get up, excuse myself, and get a drink of water or take a quick walk to let the energy run its course and not feel ashamed about that.

Unfortunately, masking often doesn't let us do that either. The embarrassment that occurs even just thinking about getting up in the middle of something important and walking out of the room, especially if we have any sort of social anxiety, can be intense enough to keep us in our seat and increase the burden.

But here's where it doesn't have to: There is a stark difference between quietly walking out of the room and running out kicking and screaming— even though it may *feel* like the same thing to the anxious mind. This is where we can rely on self-compassion and self-care to give us the permission to get up and take care of ourselves in any given moment. These are the types of accommodations we can give ourselves as adults (and often the same kinds of accommodations granted for young people in school).

I often struggle with shame and guilt that the symptoms of OCD and anxiety can cause, which is why I am prone to masking them. With OCD, the compulsion to behave in a certain way, to create rituals and habits that will ease the internal anxiety, doesn't always make sense, and it isn't always good for me and others around me. I don't want to call attention to it or be a burden to others around me, so I hide behind a mask or avoid situations that would amplify the symptoms as much as I can.

Is handwashing before you eat generally a good practice? Absolutely. Is handwashing repeatedly between every step of preparing a meal necessary? No. Is it fun for my kids to have a mother who asks a series of questions to make sure her food isn't spoiled or to ensure that no one and nothing actually touched her food so that she knows it's safe to eat? No, not fun. Is that healthy for them? Of course it isn't.

But I am compelled to ask. The questions and worrying repeat over and over in my head until I do ask. Sometimes, we take it all in good fun. "Is this *my* water?" I'll say out loud as I reach for the glass I had set down minutes prior even though I know damn well it's nobody else's, and I'll hear my kids mimic me in different funny voices from across the room. We have a good laugh, because if we took ourselves too seriously all the time, everything would hurt so much more.

I also carry a lot of shame and guilt when the rituals to help me feel safer mean that I'm not only a burden to other people but wasteful too. Cooking or preparing meals for myself in my own home is when I wash my hands the most. Before handling any new or additional food item, I wash—leaving wads of paper towels all over the counter. I try to remember to use a paper towel to open the drawers and cupboard doors so I don't have to rewash between grabbing the spatula and breaking the pasta in half over a pot of boiling water, but it's hard sometimes, and I feel badly for Mother Earth and her beautiful trees every time I yank another paper towel off the roll. Sometimes, I think I should have a separate box just to recycle all of my used paper towels. And cloth or linen towels? Not if I'm touching food. Once a cloth towel is used, it's contaminated.

Let me give you a little glimpse into what I mean. Making tomato and cucumber salad often went something like this: I would wash my hands, open the refrigerator door with the damp paper towel, and grab two Roma tomatoes out of the drawer. I would then wash off each tomato vigorously (sometimes with soap, even!) and set them on a plate. I would grab the knife and rinse that off even though it came from the drawer and hadn't been used yet. After slicing the tomato, I would reopen the refrigerator door with my pinkie finger so that the rest of my hand stayed clean as I reached for the cucumber.

With cucumber in hand, I'd head back to the sink to wash *it* off, making sure that my now-contaminated left pinkie finger didn't touch the cucumber. I'd put it aside to wash my hands again because I hadn't used the paper towel to open the refrigerator door. I would rinse off the knife, again, and slice the cucumber. I'd throw the cucumber and tomatoes into a bowl that I'd rinsed off after taking it out of the cabinet and then douse it all in an olive oil and spicy mustard mix. I'd wash my hands once more, open the silverware drawer with my right pinkie finger, and hold my left hand in a fist (the sign that it was still clean) while my right grabbed a fork. I'd rinse the fork and set it in the bowl—finally ready to sit and eat. The process can get tedious and sometimes take a very long time, making it almost too much work to bother eating.

Even though I talk openly about OCD and my "food issues" on my blog and social media, it's an entirely different experience to be in the presence of people and revealing why I'm not eating during the dinner party. If I know I will be going out with others and eating will be part of the activities, I will typically eat something at home before I go. Even beyond a few *actual* food allergies and intolerances, I feel stress when eating around others. Because I feel like I have to watch out for who is touching the food, and I'm never sure how clean the food prep process is in other people's homes, it's just easier to not eat. I'd rather enjoy the conversation and have fun with my friends than be bombarded with inner dialogue and panic about what might be lurking in the food or who touched the bread in order to plate it. But it's not without shame.

"Oh, you're not eating?"

"Did you get some food? This dish is amazing!"

"I made this without milk; I know you can't have dairy."

That last one is the hardest. When someone cooks something special just for me knowing I have food restrictions, but then I feel like I can't eat it anyway because of OCD, I feel extra guilty because they've gone and done something very considerate and I am rejecting it. So I'll generally say, "Oh, I ate a late lunch," or I'll take a little plate and move the food around. Maybe I'll even be brave enough to try a bite or two. But usually, I'll pass it off to a family member or wait until no one is watching and pitch the plate. The wastefulness is what gets me—not enough to change the behavior, but enough to make me feel like a horrible person.

So it takes work to mask, and it takes work *not* to mask and accept wherever we are in the moment. It takes effort and bravery to see ourselves more fully through the lens of self-compassion so that we don't pile additional crap on top of the fear and instead keep going in a more positive direction that makes it easier to navigate life's challenges and joys.

I had to learn ways to unmask just enough to receive the care I needed. I had to be brave enough to share more authentically with the people around me (e.g., my doctors, my family and friends, and my coworkers) to get through the day and shift the anxiety that often crept in. I had to let my guard down, show up more fully and honestly, and not try so damn hard to hide the parts of me that I deemed unworthy, weird, or downright crazy. I had to be okay with not being okay sometimes, and I'm grateful for the people who helped (and still help) me through it.

What I began to understand was that I generally underestimated the capacity of those around me to hold the space I needed. When I stopped trying so hard to hide what was happening, I was able to receive the gift of support. It was a relief, and my people loved me no matter what. Even if they were worried or frustrated by my behavior, communicating allowed me to remain more connected to my family and friends. They accepted me, flaws and all, and that allowed me to accept myself more fully as well.

Brave Reflection

How might you be masking for protection in your own life? Are you afraid of being a burden or that others will judge you? This is *so* normal. We can often feel like all eyes are on us or others are judging us if we aren't living up to the perfect (and usually unreasonable) expectations we have set ourselves up against because of upbringing, societal pressure, or cultural norms.

Take some time to write in your journal while considering the following questions:

- What would it feel like to drop the mask and move toward more acceptance of who you are in any given moment?
- What is something positive that could come with being more open and authentic with your close friends and family?
- What do you appreciate about yourself? Create a list, and start simple: "I appreciate how I care for my pet by feeding it every day" or "I appreciate that I have gotten out of bed today."

How did that go? Did you feel uncomfortable? Was it freeing? Did it leave you with more questions? All answers are okay here. If you'd like to share your insights on social media, use #EveryDay-ImBrave so that your courage can be celebrated and to serve as a reminder of the beauty inside you when times are challenging. And remember that you can head over to www.everydayimbrave.com for further information and support.

3

MISS DIAGNOSIS

WHEN PHYSICAL SYMPTOMS OF ANXIETY and fear started manifesting, I had little choice but to go see my doctor. Take one look at my medical record between December 2006 and January 2007, and the mere frequency of visits would prove to anyone that I was not well. Though I came in with symptoms such as stomach pain, pelvic pain, heart palpitations, dizziness, and frequent nausea, I walked out of the office each time without answers. A heart monitor strapped to me for a month recorded every benign heart palpitation that occurred. Ultrasounds showed nothing abnormal in my uterus or on my ovaries. The sick feeling I got every time I began to eat failed to cease with each check mark down the clean bill of health, and I was prescribed Prilosec and told that I probably just had an ulcer.

It took me a while to understand that my "illness" was more about what lay within my heart and head than in my stomach. When I was sent home from the doctor's office after three months of pain and digestive complaints with a kit to put fecal samples into test tubes, I was mortified.

In our newly remodeled bathroom in our master suite in the basement, which I rarely used, I set out all the tools on the counter. I didn't realize one could be humiliated in the privacy of her own home—while alone. *I don't have worms*, I thought. *There aren't any parasites. This is ridiculous. I will just eat.*

I returned the first soiled test tube to the Styrofoam box and wrapped it all up into the plastic hospital bag that the kit came in. After washing my hands twice, I carried the bag straight out of the house and into the garbage can, promptly throwing other trash on top of it to hide the evidence—though I wasn't really sure from whom. I then called the doctor's office and told them I wouldn't be bringing the sample in because I was better.

I continued to mask the obsessive thoughts I was having about the hidden dangers of my food, and I avoided my doctor until I got strep throat a month or so later and had to go in for antibiotics. The nurse weighed me and led me to the exam room, where she asked the standard preliminary questions and swabbed my throat.

The doctor in acute care that afternoon was not my regular doctor, nor had I been seen by him previously. But when he came in with my chart in hand, I knew he was paying attention to the numbers the minute he asked me whether I knew how much weight I'd lost since the last time I'd been there. I immediately began to cry.

Growing up, I never had much trouble with body image—not out of the norm anyway, or so it seemed. I had watched a good friend battle bulimia for a short period of time, and I'd seen *The Karen Carpenter Story* and mourned the loss of a talented musician who had starved herself to death. I'd never been one of those girls who paged through fashion magazines and looked longingly at their endless legs and dimple-free thighs. Instead, I was always the one who'd say, "Get that girl a sandwich!" and throw the magazine across the floor. I thought I was impervious to the social conditioning and media messages of standard beauty, but in reality, I just rebelled outwardly while internalizing the idea that women are more valuable if they are skinny and pretty.

When the doctor mentioned anorexia,[1] I was pretty shocked. I certainly

---

1   "Anorexia Nervosa," Mayo Clinic, updated August 9, 2024, https://www.mayoclinic.org/diseases -conditions/anorexia-nervosa/symptoms-causes/syc-20353591.

didn't think my challenges were about body image, though I couldn't deny being somewhat impressed with the amount of weight I had lost after baby number three. When my friends or family members would see me, they would comment about how good I looked for having three kids—my youngest just barely a year old at the time—and they would want to know my secret.

"Oh, yeah . . . I just changed my diet a little. I stopped eating meat and most dairy," I'd say. But I felt like a fraud. While people congratulated me on my thinning waistline and my discipline, I cringed inside. What I wanted to say, and wouldn't dare, was that I was just too scared to eat. That I was exhausted from daily rituals of washing. That my mind was so preoccupied with what other people were touching, or what my hand just brushed against, that I couldn't hold on to other important facts, like what day I needed to take the kids to the dentist or that I needed to stop at the store to get more bread for the kids' lunches.

What *was* true, however, was that I had been essentially starving myself for months, and I had convinced myself it was because I was sick. At one point, I was certain I had ovarian cancer because two of the symptoms were feeling full quickly and severe loss of appetite. I hadn't had an appetite in months. I'd feed myself only when my stomach roared—and even then, I'd only eat either a handful of naked almonds or a banana and a trail mix bar. These were safe foods that offered protein to keep me going. At least I knew I needed something to sustain myself.

But I was straddling the edge of sustainability. My clothes hung off me in all the places they once were snug. I didn't even have to unbutton my jeans anymore to remove them. I had raided my niece's giveaway pile for her trendy teenage T-shirts, needing something that would fit my hollowed frame. My bra size even went down two cups, and I saw a number on the scale that I hadn't seen since the start of puberty.

The doctor and I talked a bit about my eating habits, what I was consuming, and the stress I was under. He agreed to let my primary doctor take it from there, but he also scheduled an appointment for me with a nutritionist, who I began seeing a week later. The process of itemizing what I'd eat in a single day was embarrassing. I felt so much shame revealing what I would and wouldn't consume. The nutritionist would invite me to add some yogurt here or a vegetable I'd already outlawed there, and I'd just nod and say, "Sure," knowing full well I wasn't going to add anything. She didn't get it, though. How could she when I wasn't being fully honest? I decided to be a little more up-front next time and see where that got me.

After my second appointment with the nutritionist, I came back to work angry. I had just spent the last hour detailing a list of unsafe foods and describing how I would scrape 90 percent of the cream cheese off my bagel in case it hadn't been properly refrigerated and there was something wrong with it. Hearing myself rationalize about avoiding *E. coli* and *salmonella* in sprouts and spinach was one thing: There had been scares in the news, actual noted cases in the States, and it was understandable that I wouldn't want to eat them. But explaining that I wouldn't eat the fruit my mom had cut up and put in a bowl during our weekly Sunday dinners simply because she had touched it (after washing her hands) was an entirely different admission. There was no reason why I couldn't trust the fruit, and I felt ashamed every time I chose not to eat foods that were handled with someone's hands rather than utensils. I know it didn't make any sense and finally admitting that in the nutritionist's office made me realize just how intricate the food rules were that I had made for myself; how exhausting it was to follow them; and how uncertain, anxious, and unsafe I felt every time I sat down to have a meal.

Once back at work, I walked directly to the break room to wash my hands. I pulled the faucet handle up and to the left, pumped the soap bottle a few times, and put my hands under the water. It burned. The pain was excruciating. I looked down at my hands, frighteningly aware of the damage I was doing. My knuckles bled, my fingertips were nearly purple, and the creases along my wrists proved that my skin thirsted for health. My mom's voice from the previous week's dinner echoed in my mind. She had walked into the kitchen, having cleared a few of the kids' plates, and noticed me at the sink.

"Did you eat anything?" she asked.

"I had a piece of bread and some of the noodles," I responded.

She set the plates down on the counter next to me. I picked up the top one and began rinsing it.

She grabbed a Tupperware container and started spooning in what was left of the noodles from the pot on the stove, then stopped abruptly and faced me.

"Why are you punishing yourself?" she asked.

I turned the water off, immediately defensive. "What?"

"This thing that's going on with you," she said, "you can get help, you know."

"I *am* getting help," I insisted. "I'm still going to my therapist, and I started meeting with a nutritionist, remember?"

Sandra, my therapist at the time, was also not exactly clued in to the whole picture, though she knew I'd stopped eating meat because I thought it was making me sick. We were working through my postdivorce challenges, and she was helping me to find myself again and to reconnect to my creativity through music and writing—things I hadn't done since high school. The work was important and deeply meaningful. But I didn't really tell her about the handwashing or that there were very few foods I was even willing to try. Together, we were working on autonomy, self-identity, and trust, and this was just as important and supportive for healing—even if I hadn't yet unveiled the full scope of my fears.

My mother was silent. I didn't understand then just how hard it was to watch your adult children suffer and feel helpless to do anything about it.

As I now stood at the break room sink, her question hung in the air. *Did I need more help?* I wondered. *Was I punishing myself? If that's what this was, then why? What was I so troubled by? Was there something I'd needed to forgive? To forget?*

I didn't have any clear answers in that moment, but I knew I needed to figure out whether there was any truth to these questions and how to make this behavior stop. What I didn't yet know was that this "punishment" was actually a compulsion related to OCD. The obsessive and intrusive thoughts that what was in my food would make me sick were only quieted by the washing of hands and refusal of food. Still misdiagnosed, I continued to look for answers as to why I'd become this way.

Nothing was going to change if I wasn't willing to dig deeper, to stop masking with my providers and let them truly help me uncover the root of the issue. What were these symptoms really pointing to? Why were these fears controlling my every move?

Brave Reflection

Removing the mask took bravery, but it also demanded that I ask myself what was true about others' observations. Curiosity also allowed me to cultivate a willingness to consider an additional perspective on the symptoms that were so perplexing. My mom held up the mirror I had needed most in order to take the next steps toward acceptance and healing.

The invitation for you is to be brave enough to get curious. Where is resistance coming up for you? Is there a way you might be willing or able to listen differently to the messages and inquiries coming to you?

Furthermore, I implore you to look at this in a loving and open-hearted way. Let go of the impetus to judge, and just observe what comes up as you journal on the following questions:

- Where are you resisting support that may help you feel better? If so, are you willing to look at why that might be?

- Who might be a mirror for the medicine you need most?

- What feels like the right next step for you on the path to more self-compassion?

And please do consider reaching out to a therapist, a healer, or other mentor who might support you on the road to self-discovery, self-compassion, and healing.

If you'd like to share your insights and growth on social media, use #EveryDayImBrave so that others, too, can get curious and find a way forward through resistance. You can also go to www.everydayimbrave.com to find additional resources.

4

HISTORY LESSONS

IT TURNS OUT THAT THE TROUBLE I was having trusting what I was putting in my body had little to do with weight or illness and everything to do with safety and control. Working through some reflection exercises and conversations with Sandra about the way our bodies hold on to memory, trauma, and unexpressed emotion, I realized that I had to look back in order to move forward.

I knew I had had experiences in the past in which I'd given over bodily control, in which I allowed others to cross mental, emotional, and physical boundaries. But at this point, I thought I'd worked through most of that before I got married. However, the journey backward this time would shed more light on the truth of my experience, and learning how to reclaim control over my own body in a positive, loving way rather than through punishment was essential to the healing process.

One such exercise was a relationship history timeline, or more specifically, intimate sexual history. The complexity of being a young woman, even after the birth of the feminist movement, was confusing. Sandra had asked me to journal about my experiences and to look at intimacy, relationships, and love to gain a newer perspective than the one that blamed my teenage self for not always knowing better.

I had to uncover these moments one by one, but I wanted to do it gently and armored. Unsure what would arise or how I'd feel in the process, I chose a public space to begin because I'd be required to hold myself together. One Saturday evening, I treated myself to a night out. A coworker's husband was playing at one of my favorite local bars, and despite the snow, I went armed with a new notebook, a pocketful of self-esteem, and the energy to begin facing some deep inner challenges while listening to good music.

I got to the bar, found myself a table close to where the band had set up near the fireplace that centered the small and dimly lit room, and ordered chips and salsa with a raspberry framboise. I took my notebook out of my purse and wrote:

The first kiss.

But wait, which one was actually first? The one where the eighth-grade bully stood angrily in front of the rec center doors and wouldn't let my boyfriend and me pass the threshold until we kissed? That one? He had pressed his lips quickly to mine, his mouth closed as he gripped my hand. I don't think either of us were ready for it, and afterward, I felt shaky and sick. The atmosphere was all wrong. I ended that relationship quickly, not because I didn't like the boy but so I didn't have to worry about kissing him again.

Or was it the *other* first kiss? The one that took place on the outer edges of the high school football field near a small forest of trees? Now an eighth-grader myself, a few of the ninth-grade boys were hanging out with me and my girlfriends. They lured us into the nearby trees and joked about pretending to rape us.

"Hey, Jax, why don't we take these girls into the woods? They are obviously asking for it," Hunter called out as he took my best friend's hand in his.

Jax stifled a laugh and puffed out his chest. "Yeah," he said, grabbing me by the arm. "Let's go, woman."

I went willingly into the darkness, my friend and I giggling nervously as we were directed farther into the woods. I felt Jax lean down and gently place his mouth on mine, his warm tongue finding its way around for a few minutes before the noise around us got loud enough to make us laugh, and we exited hand in hand.

That kiss felt wonderful but also confusing. The boys using the language of rape while joking about assault (that would turn out to be an actual experience for so many of us young women in the years to come) was certainly an odd approach. I couldn't make sense of it then, and I'm not sure I can even make sense of it now. Why did they think that was funny? Why were my friends and I so willing to play along?

Both of these "first kisses" set up and strengthened a pattern of not understanding the complexities of desire and pressure, of willingness and consent, of truly knowing what it was that I desired and learning how to communicate that effectively when it came to physical and emotional intimacy.

How *was* I supposed to even know what it was I truly desired and needed at that age, anyway? As a teenage girl growing up in the '80s and early '90s, pop culture was rampant with hair bands who flaunted sexy women, objectified on cars in music videos. Movies such as *Porky's* and *Weird Science* continued to show me that women were something to be preyed on, that sex was a weapon used by people of all genders to gain control over one another.

I think about Madonna. I idolized her for her fierceness, the freedom with which she carried herself and owned her music and her image. She was bold and brave, and I honor that still, yet here I was at ten years old singing "Like a Virgin" and working on my sexy eye gaze. When I look back on all of this, something just doesn't add up, and it sent such a bizarre message out to the world. How were we to reconcile not being too sexy so we didn't attract the male gaze in a harmful way with being sexy enough to show others we had what they wanted? Why is it always about the "other" in the first place? What about our own desires? How about the mixed messages that the "good girl" is the one boys marry whereas the "bad girl" is the one boys take to bed? Where is the middle ground? Mix in Judeo-Christian societal sex guilt and parents and teachers telling you sex is frowned upon, and you've got some pretty unclear answers about why you enjoy the feel of that redhead's lips on the back of your neck but want to throw up when the blond sticks his tongue in your mouth.

And what about love? How were you supposed to know what was love and what was just a ploy to get into someone's pants? Drop in hormones, movie dramas, and the fact that some of the other girls in your high school were already "doing it," and you've got one mixed-up little girl.

I want to add here, too, that this is all very heteronormative focused. Even though I believe sexuality and gender are a spectrum and I'm likely somewhere in the middle of it, I grew up in an era that focused mostly on heterosexuality. I cannot speak to the experience otherwise, though I know there are complexities there as well. Social media, pop culture, religion, and the news can do a number on us all—especially when it comes to sex.

Because of these mixed messages, this meant I had no idea what I really wanted. Did I want Curtis to put his hand up my shirt? Well, yeah, if it meant that he'd hang out with me a little longer. Did I want Blake to kiss me in the middle of downtown for all to see? Yes, because it let others know he was mine. Did I want to take my pants off in the spare bedroom during a house party? Nope. But I did it anyway because I didn't want to be that girl who left a guy hanging.

And actually, it's not that simple. None of it is, because I also wanted to experience the joy of touch; I wanted to experience connection and love. I wanted to know what it felt like to gaze into another's eyes and feel our bodies together. I wanted to feel warm, excited, and joyful. But I didn't know how to communicate any of that. It often felt like a lose–lose situation in which I was wrong for feeling frisky *and* I was wrong for being frisked.

What I didn't understand was how playing the role of rebellious, sexy teenager would disguise what I truly wanted—and how harmful it would be for me in the long run. I didn't want to be judged for having sexual feelings and curiosity, but I also thought that if I loved a boy enough, everything in the world would be all right. I was a hopeless romantic, yearning for something intangible.

A few moments from this particular trip down memory lane stand out. What is important here is twofold:

One—that I understand why I behaved the way I did and why I believed the things I did as a teenager navigating relationships and sex, but also that I can have self-compassion for the girl who needed to feel love and was innately curious.

Two—that I do better now. Having seen these patterns play out again and again, I can become better at understanding my own needs, thoughts, and desires and communicating them.

What I also uncovered in the process of digging into my history was that 2006 was not the first time in my life that I'd stopped eating. The summer before my junior year of high school had been full of drama and excitement. It was 1992, and I had spent my evenings chasing older boys who had just graduated and were only looking for short-term rendezvous until they left for college. My friends and I would smoke cigarettes and ride around in cars after dark. I tried my first beer and went cliff jumping at the nearby lake. Shock and sadness rippled through our community when one of our own put a shotgun in his mouth and didn't look back. We all came together sleepless and hungry for answers in the weeks following our classmate's death. It would change us all, but especially those closest to him. I think about him often, still.

Then, one night, I got a phone call that this kid I'd had a crush on earlier that year was back in town for a few days visiting. I drove over to the apartment where he was staying and hung out with him and his friends for a bit until, one by one, they left and Darren and I were alone.

He took another beer out of the fridge and came back to the living room to sit with me. I'm not sure how many drinks he'd already had; I'd had one and declined a second. Darren was intriguing to me, newly eighteen, smart, sexy, and experienced. I knew I was playing with fire, and that had excited me, but when we moved from the couch to the floor and it was clear where this was heading, I suddenly realized, as he unbuttoned his jeans, that this was not at all what I wanted. Not like this, and not with him.

"Wait," I whispered, trying to prop myself up on my elbows and hold my tank top down. His hands were persistent. "No, I . . ."

"Come on," he insisted. "We've been talking around this all night." He kissed me again, his hands roaming farther down, the weight of his legs pressing against mine.

"I don't . . ." He tugged my skirt up. "I can't . . ." My voice fell away. I felt like I started disappearing inside myself. *I want him to like me, remember? I want to be grown up. I want to explore this, don't I? It would be rude to stop now. He'd be so angry. He'd laugh at me.*

I started to shiver in the July heat, and I closed my eyes when he reached for a condom he'd stashed in the pocket of his jeans, now crumpled on the floor. The carpet felt rough underneath me, the skin on my back now exposed. My head tapped the glass of the sliding door behind me with each movement above me.

"Man, it's like slamming my dick into a brick wall," he said, and then moments later, it was over.

I didn't stay long enough to even notice that I was bleeding. I drove home, took a shower, and never spoke to Darren again.

When school started a month later, everything felt different. I was going through the motions of everyday life: attending school, preparing for show choir auditions and rehearsals, spending Friday nights out with the girls. But at night, all alone, I couldn't get settled. I was irritated and angry, and I'd sit in front of my mirror and not recognize myself. There was a guttural ache deep inside me that I couldn't name and that I certainly didn't want to feed. The only solace I found was with the *scritch scratch* on my skin from the paring knife I'd taken from the kitchen one evening—not enough pressure to bleed, but just enough to scar.

Physical pain was easier to bear than the darkness that swirled around in my mind. It was something I could control, start, and stop whenever I wanted, just like food. I had no appetite as I hurled words of shame and fury at myself, because some part of me believed that I didn't deserve to eat, to feel nourished. I was already full of damage, and self-harm seemed like the only way to quiet the screams inside my head and numb the pain. I didn't want to die; self-harm and suicidal ideation are not the same. Instead, I wanted to control the pain.

As time went on, I didn't hunger for anything and watched gleefully as I shed pounds. I wasn't overweight to begin with, but nearly every teenage girl I knew thought that they were a little bit fat if they had natural curves instead of pencil-thin legs and bellies that rolled instead of creased. I distinctly remember boasting about my 104-pound number on the scale to the boy who was my close friend and soon-to-be boyfriend, Darcy, as we walked from our government class to the choir room.

"What? No way," he said. "104? I can lift way more than that."

"No, you can't," I rolled my eyes. Within seconds, he had me in the air, and we laughed as he carried me the rest of the way, plopping me down in my assigned seat as the bell rang.

Darcy and I had met in junior high, both members of the rival school show choirs; we connected through music and performing. Or more aptly, we watched each other on stage, and I giggled a lot. He wasn't your typical show choir kid, but he loved music, and there weren't a lot of options back then to be involved. In high school, a small core group of friends bonded over summer shenanigans: three boys from across town, two of whom were a year older and could drive, and a few of us girls from the west side. We would spend most of our days at Maggie's house because her parents both worked and we were often left to our own devices. We would hit the pool or drive around to pick up our other friends and head to Dane's Dairy, the ice cream shop where we all worked a few hours a week because it was the only job we could have at fourteen and fifteen. The pay was crap, but the ice cream was phenomenal and often free for us.

One particular warm summer day stands out in my memory as a time when I first began to feel closer to Darcy. We had decided to bike to what we called the "Rez," the water reservoir with a small beach generally lined with cigarette butts and disgusting water that stained our bathing suits. It was only about three miles out of town, and we loaded up our backpacks with our suits, snacks, and plenty of water. The boys were active and biked often. The girls and I, however, not so much, but my friends were generally in better shape than me, seeing as I was already smoking cigarettes while crouched and hiding along the side of my house. I'm not sure why I thought I could make this bike trip, but I didn't want to be left out, so I gave it a shot.

We took the main roads out to Dubuque Street, which became long and windy the farther out of town we got. I was losing steam pretty quickly, and the rest of the group was far ahead. Never being one with much stamina (I had always walked the four-minute mile in gym class, which took more like fourteen minutes), I knew I was doomed as they sped farther away and up a steep hill. Darcy looked back, saw me struggling, and took a quick U-turn on his bike down to meet me. I was stopped by then, barely balancing and totally out of breath.

"Here, gimme your backpack," he said, reaching out his hand. I watched as he emptied the contents of my bag into his own and balled up the bag to fit it inside his as well.

"I don't think I can do this," I said. And, since it was the early 1990s, I didn't have a cell phone to call someone for a ride. I was going to be stuck right there in the middle of the county road on a hot day in July, when the humidity often hits 100 percent.

"Yes, you can," Darcy encouraged as he slung his bag back over his shoulders. "Just hang on to my backpack and let me do the work." I chuckled, skeptical that this would actually get me anywhere, but I put my feet back on the pedals of my ten-speed, balanced one hand toward the middle of the handlebars, and reached the other out to grab hold of the backpack now strapped to his body.

He pedaled, we lurched forward a bit, and I let out a little yelp. But Darcy kept pedaling, and I righted myself as he chugged us both up that hill. I couldn't believe it, and I was grateful that he refused to leave me behind. This was the kind of guy Darcy was. He would continue to show up for me and his friends in kind ways like this over the years.

It was shortly after he carried me down the hallway that fall that our friendship started to shift. He had already asked another girl to go to the homecoming dance with him, and I found myself feeling mighty jealous. We continued to talk as friends, but it became obvious to us both, in the quiet moments and more frequent phone calls, that there was something more there.

One crisp late-October evening, after the rest of our friends left our typical after-dinner homework hangout, Darcy lingered a bit longer in my room. When it was time for him to go, I slipped on a light sweater and walked him out to his car—a Pontiac Firebird, dark tones and real sleek. The night sky was clear enough to see Orion's Belt, and as I took in the view, I realized I wanted nothing more than for him to kiss me at that moment.

In true '80s rock fashion, I slipped myself between him and the driver's side door, blocking his entrance and looking up at the star-filled sky. I don't have any recollection of the words we exchanged, but our intentions were clear, and he leaned in toward me—first for a gentle, slow touch of the lips that then, once requited, built from there. I was already, and instantly, in love.

His was the best first kiss I'd ever had, our years of friendship sparking something I didn't know could exist: a foundation of intimacy that was created from a mutual connection and care for one another, not just because of teenage hormones, proximity, or conquest. It was a new and different experience at the time, and everything that passed between us felt more meaningful as a result. I had wanted this one to stick more than anything.

Romance bloomed as winter approached, and for a few sweet months, all was right in the world. However, as the weather got colder and the days got shorter, I became pretty depressed—partially because winter was always hard, but also because I began feeling needy and overbearing within the relationship, and I couldn't put my finger on why. I couldn't communicate what was wrong most of the time, and that became increasingly difficult for maintaining any sort of connection.

Even though I couldn't articulate it at the time, I know now that I was struggling so much because of what had happened on the apartment floor months earlier. Somewhere deep down, I couldn't reconcile how much it had affected me. It wasn't until decades later that I understood that I felt like a part of me had betrayed my body and ruined a piece of myself. Even more, I realized I was having a really hard time forgiving that naive and reckless girl who willingly put herself in the path of potential danger. I raged against the part of me that didn't speak loudly enough and didn't demand that he stop; that didn't just get up and leave when or if she had had the chance; that gave up, gave in, and would continue to do so in different ways for years to come in order to avoid conflict.

With that confusion juxtaposed against the positive intimacy I'd now experienced falling in love with my friend, I ended up placing so much of my own value there. I trusted him, and I felt like he made me whole again after someone else had taken a piece of me. I was eating again, and I felt better most days, but I was also scared that I wouldn't be able to move through the darkness if anything happened to Darcy because I thought he was the one who had brought back the light in my world. Looking back, it is crystal clear that that is why I thought I needed him so badly.

That's also *a lot* of subconscious pressure to place on a nearly seventeen-year-old young man. He didn't know this particular experience had happened to me, and I certainly couldn't verbalize it or even realize how the trauma would infiltrate our relationship at the time. I didn't want to think about it, nor did I know how to talk about it. I wanted Darcy to love me and continue to love me, but I couldn't explain how damaged I felt inside. The worse I felt, the more I tried to control our relationship, and I became clingy and irritable until it all unraveled.

I continued to love him, desperately and alone for months after we broke up, and I began cutting again—just a little bit to try to relieve the emotional pain I'd been experiencing. I had carved his initials into the delicate skin on my left breast, right over my heart. It was desperate and dramatic, and it would take more than ten years for the scarring to disappear enough not to be seen in the sunlight. I carried on day to day in a haze. My grades slipped, my friendships suffered, and my typical depressive symptoms were not easily overlooked.

I had wanted to be in this state of longing and loneliness because it was easier than facing the anger and rage of an experience I didn't even know was rape. I thought it was just stupid teenage sex; I thought I was the only one to blame. As a result, I struggled through the remainder of my teen years and into adulthood to find that balance between love and lust, between trust and deceit, between control and powerlessness. I struggled to understand myself as a sexual person, being comfortable in my own skin and being okay with that, rather than feeling like sex was for reasons other than expressing love.

It took me more than ten years and two different therapists to be able to even call it date rape. I was utterly ashamed because I felt I had put myself in a situation that I probably *could* have escaped from and didn't. I gave up and gave in because I was too afraid of what would have happened if I got up and left in the middle of it all. I couldn't make sense of it; I couldn't forgive myself; I couldn't dampen the discomfort.

So at sixteen, I had stopped eating. It was the only way I could manage the trauma of what had occurred on that apartment floor—the only way I could try to take back control of my body when someone else had taken so much from me in an instant. And it wasn't the last time I would try to take back control through food.

Unveiling these truths with my therapist Sandra as an adult allowed me to see my past from a different perspective. I understood that my behaviors, feelings, and choices were what helped me feel safer in my mind and body. By looking back, I could see each relationship and intimate experience through a whole different lens, and I understood that knowing, understanding, and acknowledging the past was step one. Step two would be to begin making choices that reflected what I'd learned from this unfolding. It took bravery to look back, and it would take even more courage to move forward.

Brave Reflection

As we take time to look back at our history and uncover some of the root causes of our fears and behaviors, we must observe them with curiosity and an open heart. It's important to recognize that we can learn from our experiences, and if we don't like how we showed up on any given day, we can do better next time. I had to learn to forgive the parts of me that didn't know any better as a teenager, and in doing so, I began to ask myself how I might forgive the younger parts of me and move forward.

We can find it challenging to forgive ourselves—even more so than forgiving others. The weight of regret holds us back from moving forward. We have to return to these moments and those parts of ourselves with compassion, to care about the part of us that may have felt afraid or confused.

Consider the following journal prompts, and begin with the one that most resonates. You can return to each of these time and again:

- How can you show love to the parts of you that might feel anger, shame, or guilt?
- How can you forgive the parts of you that you wish had done things differently?
- How can you show up differently, today, if that's what you desire to do?

When you bravely look back, new perspectives, feelings, and ideas can bubble up to the surface. These can be helpful in moving forward from a more learned place. If you'd like to share your process and insights on social media, use #EveryDayImBrave so that you can light the pathway for others doing the inner work too. There are also additional resources at www.everydayimbrave. com for support.

5

PICKING UP THE PIECES

AFTER A DISASTER OR SOME SORT OF nature-made upheaval, there is a time when you step back and survey the destruction. About a year after Nick moved out of the house, we had a pretty significant, though brief, storm. It toppled over trees and power lines across the neighborhood, and pieces of my roof were ripped off. I took pictures of the scattered tiles around my backyard and made the appropriate calls to the insurance company. The kids and I piled up all the tiles we could find and set them in the garage. I was thankful that the roof was mostly intact and there was no water leaking into the house. For the most part, the rest of the cleanup and repair process was out of my hands: My dad took care of meeting with the roofers later in the week while I was at work, and a few days later, it was fixed, and I didn't have to pay a dime.

The aftermath of divorce, however, is more complex. There are no insurance companies to call and no cleanup crew. Even after all was said and done in the courthouse and we were living under different roofs, the debris was still scattered across my house, and it became very difficult to find the time and motivation to pick through it, categorize it, and decide what would stay or go.

Over time, things that were once "ours" were relegated to the basement storage room. It was a mess. Mismatched boxes sprawled everywhere, and piles of random stuff were just lying on the floor: photo albums, books, kids' items that they had outgrown, and even scrapbook supplies stowed away for a project that would never come to fruition.

One evening, I went into the storage room to look at my old computer, a Gateway my parents had bought me when I was a single parent living with them while in graduate school. I had gotten out of bed to see if my old PC had an ethernet port in it—having had some idea about connecting it to my cable modem and hooking it up to my wireless router so that I could carry my Mac laptop around with me. Finding nothing but a modem port—which I already knew was busted—I stood and stared at the mess around me.

I shuffled a few things around and found a book that I'd taken from my mom's shelf years ago: Kahlil Gibran's *The Prophet*. She had bought it early on in her relationship with my dad and written an inscription of love, designing a beautiful future. I flipped through the pages and came upon Gibran's teachings on marriage, which I had first read before I ever met Nick.

Gibran talks of allowing space within togetherness, letting the "winds of the heavens dance between you."[1] He also talks of individual strength, saying that "the pillars of the temple stand apart / And the oak tree and the cypress grow not in each other's shadow."[2] This was the kind of marriage I had always longed for—one in which two people were free to be fully themselves, to have space in which to move and be, yet connected deeply to the other under one roof. And yet this was not the marriage I had participated in, nor did I truly know how to cocreate it at the time. What I did know is that I have always longed for space in relationships, feeling oppressed by the nature of what I thought commitment meant, a dislike for the word *compromise*, a rebellion against togetherness—and yet I was

---

1   Kahlil Gibran, *The Prophet* (Knopf, 1923), 19.

2   Gibran, *The Prophet*, 20.

lonely, and I came into this relationship with unmet needs that took me years to understand.

Additionally, my individual strength had waxed and waned over the years, and by the time I had gained back some semblance of empowerment and self-advocacy, learning more about who I was and how I wanted to be in the world, I was no longer the woman who had said "I do." That shift was a large part of our undoing.

I put Gibran's book down and picked up a thick baby blue photo album—our son's newborn photos. Nick and I looked like two very different people than the ones we had become. He was young and vibrant, looking excited and hopeful. I was about thirty pounds over the thirty pounds of baby weight I had put on and looked exhausted, like a shell of myself. My son's beautiful face, with his bright brown eyes and gummy smile, couldn't shake the trepidation with which I held the photos in my hands.

I didn't want to look at them. I didn't want to remember. The grief of a promised future now gone was too much to bear. I would later understand that the anxiety and OCD symptoms that had me constantly checking and rechecking my surroundings for anything that might have contaminated the food or the air around us were part of what caused a big rift. It would look like control, nagging, questioning. It would create arguments, more fear, and bigger, stronger walls. I felt guilty, ashamed that these actions were part of the undoing. But I also felt solid in our decision to divorce: We'd stayed friends and family, and I was learning to hold both the promise of new beginnings and the grief of change at once.

As I set the photo album back down, I turned to see the rails of the crib leaning against the back wall. Taken down nearly two years prior, after my youngest transitioned to a toddler bed, I wasn't sure why I was keeping it. I was definitely done having kids. I walked closer to the crib and gingerly ran my fingers across the top bar.

In July of 2006, Lily was born, weighing in at seven pounds and some-odd ounces. She fit immediately into the family mold. She was a relatively easy infant, content to watch the activity around her and barely batting an eye when the dog would lick her as he walked by the bouncy seat. She fussed a little when bored or overstimulated but screeched like a pterodactyl when hunger struck. My older daughter, Shelby, was eight years old and kept my then-two-year-old son, Evan, entertained with games and stories. I was often impressed with her patience and grateful for all the ways she helped our now family of five run.

When I was still pregnant, Nick had remodeled the basement and created a master suite for us in our little house. I was terribly apprehensive about being downstairs while the kids were on the main floor sleeping. I wanted to be just footsteps away in case they needed something. But we needed a room of our own, and we had disagreed about the two younger children sharing a room.

So we had given our eldest a walkie-talkie to communicate with me between floors. We had a baby monitor for our toddler, and the baby slept in her bassinet next to me for the first couple of months. Eventually, we transitioned Evan out of his crib and into the toddler bed and set Lily up in the crib in her own room. Simultaneously, I began sleeping upstairs again in Lily's new room, where we kept a bed and her crib. I was afraid of Evan walking the stairs at night, fearing he might fall and hurt himself in a half-asleep state. This way, if he needed anything, he could toddle over right down the hall instead of sleepily maneuvering the stairs. Lily would sleep in the crib for most of the night, and then, after a 2:00 a.m. feeding, we'd cuddle up until the alarm went off at 6:00 to start our day.

At one point, angry and frustrated that I wasn't continuing to sleep in the master bedroom, Nick took the extra bed out of Lily's room and put it in the garage. When two young and stubborn personalities get together, it can make for some interesting dynamics. His checkmate move didn't work, though. I began sleeping on the couch in the front room near the kids' bedrooms instead. Rational or not, being near my kids during the night was something I wasn't willing to compromise on, and underneath that was another truth: that I preferred to sleep alone.

Years later, standing in my basement, I chuckled a little to myself. The kids and I still often played musical beds (instead of musical chairs) in the middle of the night because I'd fallen asleep reading to them or someone had a bad dream. Sleeping alone rarely happened.

I let go of the crib and made a mental note to donate or sell it. As I turned to exit the storage room, I noticed the red and gold glass drinking goblets that had been surrounded in bubble wrap since our move back to Iowa nearly six years prior sitting on the shelf near the light switch. They were from Pier 1 Imports: tall glass champagne flutes with a deep red coloring at the base and gold painted designs weaved around the glass. I had bought them a year before Nick and I met because they reminded me of the gorgeously intricate henna designs young Indian women paint on their hands and feet before their weddings. I wanted to drink from these glasses on my future wedding day; I wanted the flutes to represent the beginning of a uniquely beautiful and rich relationship.

I wasn't the kind of girl who had spent a lot of time dreaming up her perfect wedding day—collecting ideas for dresses and picking out color schemes. In fact, for much of my young adult life, I was pretty certain I was never even going to get married. I couldn't fathom what life would be like with that kind of commitment, but these glasses were magnificent, so I had bought them. And months later, when I became engaged and began planning a wedding, these glasses became the centerpiece I was going to work around.

But I didn't end up having that wedding. I had a much different one. There was no red and gold. There was no massive celebration party. Instead, I wore blue and white and laughed nervously through my vows as our immediate family looked on. We had lunch at a restaurant that put us down for the wrong date in their calendar, and we had to wait in the lobby as they set up a table for fifteen in the middle of a crowded room the day after Christmas. I had brought the goblets with me—along with some sparkling cider because I was nearing the twelve-week mark, pregnant with my son—and the family all toasted the beginning of our next adventure.

But just two days later, the adventure had turned into a marital screaming match. In a fit of anger, I threw my keys at our apartment wall and shattered the chain of beads that my then-five-year-old daughter had made for me—my name spelled out in block letters now strewn about the floor. She and I picked up the beads, each of us in tears, as my new husband locked himself in the back bedroom. (Recently, all three of us on different occasions have said that that day marked the time when we knew in our hearts that this wasn't going to work.)

That night in my basement, as I pondered the bravery it took to embark on new beginnings, I unwrapped the glasses and gingerly ran my fingers along the sides to follow the golden swirls. I cried a little. I was also tempted to throw them and watch them shatter—a dream lost, a symbol of something that never was. Instead, I carried them out of the storage room into my office nook and placed them on the window sill.

The glasses gave me a bit of hope that a relationship allowing for both togetherness and space can exist, especially if I consciously work to make that happen. The flutes were tall, elegant. They looked strong, and yet they were fragile—much like my own heart was at the time. And in their new setting, they stood apart like Gibran's pillars so that the "winds of the heavens danced between" them and the strength of hope was restored.

Brave Reflection

It takes ongoing reflection to live a more conscious and deliberate life. When you have that gut feeling that something isn't working out in a way that's best for you or aligned, it's important to acknowledge that small quiet voice inside that's letting you know something needs to change, even when it's hard to hear. Pay attention to how you feel, use mindfulness tools to get present, and as you pick up the pieces of the aftermath of any big change, take the opportunity to choose what to take with you and what to let go of.

It takes bravery to look at how things went wrong and learn from them, to rebuild from a place of knowing what is right for you in the present moment, even if that's changed from the past. You are constantly evolving, and the lesson here is to allow yourself the time and space to reflect. Use the following journal prompts to support your process:

- How can you return to yourself in order to recognize what's best for you at this time?

- What are the pieces of your past that you wish to let go of? What is no longer serving you as you move forward and create more of what you desire to experience in your life?

- How can you continue to consciously create more of what you desire, even as you move through a challenging time?

If you'd like to share your intentions of what you are letting go of and how you want to move forward on social media, use #EveryDayImBrave so that others on the journey can hold and support your vision for the future. Remember that you can also go to www.everydayimbrave.com to find additional resources and support.

6

UNGROUNDED

WHILE MY NEW BOYFRIEND ANDREW'S CAR sat empty and unused in my driveway, awaiting his return from an international work trip, my ex-husband, Nick, was back in my home, temporarily sleeping in the basement for a few weeks after a breakup with his live-in girlfriend. By October, Nick would be gone, having accepted a job a few states away and hoping the space would provide him with a much-needed new outlook. His leaving would mark a new era for our children, as they negotiated living with a long-distance father, and I knew the change would affect each of them in different ways.

I also knew I would have to continue to rely on the strength that had gotten me through each big change in my life previously. That strength comes from a profound belief that good will prevail—that despite the everyday fears and phobias I'd been dealing with, I couldn't spend my time fretting about what *could* happen when he left; I had to rest in the knowledge of what *was* happening and how I would choose to deal with it.

What was happening was a shift in our family dynamics. Despite our differences, I knew that Nick was a good man who loved his children deeply and who was making the choice that he believed was going to help him heal and become a better version of himself. I knew that our children would survive, not without bumps and bruises but with a whole lot of wisdom. And

I knew that I had a community of friends and family who would continue to help me care for them daily. I knew that at the end of the day, what mattered most would be how I chose to react to the change, how I helped my children move forward while staying connected to their dad over the miles.

My children would take cues from me on how to manage the transition. I did my best to hold space for all their feelings that would arise. I also tried to show them strategies to express those emotions and then shift their focus back toward their schooling, their creative pursuits, and whatever was present in the moment. It wasn't always easy, for any of us, but we'd stayed in constant communication with their dad through phone and video calls as much as we could. Some nights, there was very little sleeping to be had. Lily was only four years old at the time and would often cry herself to sleep as I rubbed her back, only to wake again hours later and crawl into my bed for comfort.

A month or so after Nick left, I had a pretty severe panic episode at work that seemed to come out of nowhere. By this time, I'd left the classroom and was working an educational corporate job that allowed me a little more flexibility and a lot more money—both things needed for a single-parent household. It was just before noon, and I had started feeling lightheaded and kind of out of it. I figured it was probably low blood sugar; I'd only had coffee and a banana for breakfast and a Tootsie Pop as a midmorning snack. I warmed up a protein-packed veggie burger and ate it voraciously in my cubicle, then waited for the weird feeling to fade. When it didn't, I started to worry. My heart raced faster, my fingers and toes tingled, and I couldn't really tell where my body began and ended. My breath quickened, and I got up to walk to my friend Shanti's cubicle just a few steps down the hall. I felt like I was falling over, like the walls were caving in, but I made it to the extra chair by her desk. Once seated, I was afraid to move again.

I tried the tools I'd been using for years in an attempt to calm myself down: I focused on Shanti's voice as she talked to me and counted my breath in cycles of four while I massaged my neck with my thumb over the carotid artery to try to slow my heart rate.

I tried to distract myself from what was occurring inside my body by attempting to help Shanti with the work she was doing on her computer. I tried to read the words on her screen, but each time, a new wave of fog passed through me, and my sense of panic rose again. I couldn't hold myself together any longer, and I started to cry right there in cubicle land for all passersby to see.

Another coworker stopped to see whether I was okay, and I tried to shoo him away, but it was clear by the shaking, crying, and disorientation that I wasn't okay. He decided to call the first responders support team in the building, and one of them came to look me over. I felt so embarrassed as he took my blood pressure and asked me a line of questions to assess my cognitive function, which was totally fine. However, as ridiculous as I felt, I was also relieved: Someone else was in charge for the moment. They were figuring out the best next steps; they would help me understand what was wrong and how to fix it. I had been so busy being strong that I didn't realize what the pressure was doing to me. I had become totally ungrounded, the stress of constantly handling it all making me feel like I had lost my footing, with no strong foundation to stand on.

Once finished with the initial assessment, the medic decided that I should go see the doctor just to make sure everything was okay. I didn't feel comfortable enough to drive, so I called my mom, who left her own busy workplace to come get me. Shanti walked me out to the car, my arm cradled in the crook of hers, and I cried even more as I buckled myself into the passenger seat. The little girl in me needed her mom, relieved by the safe space where I was allowed, finally, to break a little more.

When we reached the doctor's office, I was steady but still weak. The physician ordered some tests, and I waited for blood work while the nurse hooked me up to a portable EKG machine that measured the electrical pulses of my heart. Everything turned up perfectly fine.

My mom dropped me off at home and left to pick up my kids from school and take them out to dinner with my dad, who then picked up my car from the office and drove it back to my house so I'd have it for the morning.

As I rested on the couch, Shanti texted me: *Feeling any better yet? Call or text when you can.*

I replied, *I'm okay. Thanks for helping me today. I think I just overdid the "I can handle this myself" bit. My parents are helping with the kids tonight so I can rest. I'll see you in the morning.*

Shanti: *I'll be there. You know I got you, girl!*

Me: *Love you, so thankful for you!*

Shanti: *Love you, too.*

At that moment, I realized I didn't have to wait until it was an emergency to ask for help. I was so grateful for my friend, my family, and the team of medics and doctors who ensured I was indeed physically okay so that I could tackle what weighed heavy on my heart. I had to learn how to ask for what I needed, to speak it out loud so that I could open up to more love and trust in others' support—something I didn't do on that apartment floor as a teenager and that I rarely did in my first marriage. I was finally beginning to understand just how important it was to stop pretending I was okay. I needed to handle myself with as much care as I was handling my children through the shift of their dad moving away. I needed to ground myself and find relief for my spinning thoughts, to do better than vending machine lunches, and to treat my stiff and trembling body better in order to feel more centered, brave, and equipped to care for my family.

I also realized that I wasn't even relying on Andrew, my boyfriend, because I wanted to be fiercely independent and try not to care that he was often away. Yet I had to admit, if only to myself, that I was feeling pretty isolated and alone. My parents continued to be the solid bedrock on which I could lean. I was torn between feeling indebted to them and grateful, as well as knowing that each carpool, meal, and bedtime routine they helped with led to a deeper, more meaningful relationship with their grandchildren. And so I continued to show up to my corporate education job and show up more fully present for my family, and I began to make the most of this new normal.

I had a follow-up appointment with my doctor a week or so later to check in. We went through some standard procedures, such as blood work to double-check my iron and Vitamin D levels (often associated with anxiety and depression), and then I recounted what had happened at work.

"So would you say these are feelings of dissociation?" my doctor began.

"Yeah, like I look at my hands, and I'm wondering if they actually belong to my body," I responded.

"Yes, that's dissociation. How often would you say this is happening?" she pressed.

"Maybe a couple times a week?" I said. "Or like the floor beneath me is uneven or falling . . . that happens a lot."

"Well, I definitely think that you're under a lot of stress right now. This is probably contributing to the more potent anxiety you're feeling. I think it's important that we consider medication that could help, and I'd like to get you in to see a therapist," she said, turning back toward the computer in the exam room and clicking away as I spoke.

"I was working with a therapist, but I haven't seen her in a couple years," I told her. "And I don't think I can take medicine."

"You don't think you *can*?" she paused mid-keystroke and looked at me, a little confused.

"Well, I mean I am physically able," I clarified, "but I don't want to." I didn't admit that I was scared of taking any medications, especially psych drugs. I support anybody's personal choices about taking medications, but it just wasn't something I wanted to do.

"Hmmm," she took a moment to think. "Well, if you don't want to take medications to help bring down this anxiety, there are some specific therapies that can help with panic attacks like this." She turned back to the computer and clicked a few more buttons. "I'm going to send a referral over to our behavioral health department, but I'm going to get in contact with one of their providers who I'd like you to see." She wrote down an email on the bottom of my checkout papers. "I'm not sure if he is taking new patients; he's usually pretty full," she told me. "But he is also a friend of mine, and I'll send him a note to see if he is able to work you in sooner rather than later."

"Okay," I replied and took the papers she handed me. "Thank you."

"You're welcome, and if you need anything in the meantime, just send me a message," she said.

I was grateful for the extra time and attention my doctor had given me. One of the things that depression and anxiety can do is make you feel like a burden to others. *Don't believe this lie.* Call the doctor's office. Reach out to a mentor. Send that text you've been writing and rewriting to your friend. Be brave enough to tell others, "Today has been hard, and I could use some support." You'll be amazed at the love and care that come back to you, and I encourage you to be open to receiving it.

For me, becoming more open to support meant that I would start with a new therapist a few weeks later. Using different therapy techniques from before, I'd return to the inner work so that I wouldn't just get through the days but rise above the challenges with my feet firmly planted on the ground.

Brave Reflection

When what we've been doing to keep anxiety at bay isn't enough, we have to be brave enough to call in reinforcements, to try new and different ways to help ourselves feel better and function better in our day-to-day.

My invitation here is to take some time to journal about your support team. Who are the friends or family who you can ask to have at your side when things are tougher than usual? Who are the practitioners, mentors, or guides who can help you see new perspectives and feel more supported on your journey of self-discovery? Use the following fill-in-the-blank sentences as journal prompts:

- When I am feeling most challenged by the stressors in my life, I can turn to _____ for support.

- The services, podcasts, books, and people in my life that I can return to when times are hard are _____ _____.

- When I need support the most, it is difficult to _____ _____, but I can be brave and reach out to receive that support.

If you are feeling alone in this, please reach out to a therapist, a doctor, or your local crisis hotline. You matter, and there is support available, even if it *feels* like there isn't. There are resources and support available at www.everydayimbrave.com. And if you'd like to share on social media how being open to support is part of your brave work, use #EveryDayImBrave so that others can lift you up on your most challenging days.

7

EMBRACING THE TIGER

IN ONE OF OUR FIRST MEETINGS, Dr. Temple talked about a book titled *Why Zebras Don't Get Ulcers*, in which the author, Robert Sapolsky, examines the science of stress-related diseases that only humans (and certainly not zebras!) endure. The short, short version of the story Sapolsky tells goes like this:[1] Zebra is peacefully grazing when Tiger attacks. Zebra senses Tiger, gets a surge of adrenaline, and runs. Zebra escapes Tiger and lives another day.

Now, the next time Zebra goes to graze, you might think that he says to himself, *Well, the last time I was out there, Tiger nearly got me! Maybe I shouldn't go out and graze today. It's just too dangerous. That Tiger could be out there.*

But no, Zebra doesn't avoid going out to graze. Sure, Zebra might look around with an awareness that Tiger might come, but Zebra still goes out there. He still eats, because to a zebra, the tiger is only real when the zebra can see it, smell it, and hear it.

Ironically, it is *because* our brains can remember the past and project into the future that these sorts of physical symptoms of ongoing anxiety can be

---

1   Robert M. Sapolsky, "Why Don't Zebras Get Ulcers?," chap. 1 in *Why Zebras Don't Get Ulcers*, 1st ed. (W. H. Freeman and Company, 1994).

created. Our powerful minds can create physiological responses to something that isn't actually occurring in the present. We are amazing! And yet this gift also presents us with a situation in which we have to navigate that power. Being present in the moment is often the best and only remedy for worry.

Unlike the zebra, I had *literally* stopped eating for a while. That tiger started showing up in myriad ways and would set off my internal alarm system. It would roar in my ears in the kitchen when the wooden spoon touched the countertop while cooking. It would sprawl on the couches of my friend's house during potlucks, its eyes fixated on me as I moved about the room.

Tiger would show up in other ways too: on the middle of a bridge, the fifth floor of a building, the glass elevator, the stadium full of people. Tiger would block my entry to an airplane, a boat, or a bus. Tiger would follow me everywhere I turned, no matter how hard I tried to push it away, yell in its face, or run away. If Tiger was going to stick around, then I had to start seeing and accepting it for what it was: *imaginary.*

Despite how real panic feels, how much my knees give out or my heart races, or how the lump in my throat grows and I begin to feel separate from my body, these feelings I experience are often a reaction to a threat that isn't truly there. The likelihood of falling over the railing of a second-story balcony is slim. The numbers have shown[2] that plummeting to the ground during a routine commercial flight is actually extremely rare. And certainly my silverware doesn't need to be rinsed off when I take it out of the kitchen drawer, just in case. But how was I going to reconcile the very real physical symptoms with the imaginary danger that I could barely consciously register?

On the way home from my first appointment, I stopped to pick up my kids from the after-school program. Once buckled in, Lily pulled the new panda bear stuffed animal she'd gotten from Andrew out of her backpack.

---

2 Jordan Blake, "How Many Commercial Planes Crash a Year?," *Bitlux* (blog), May 9, 2024, https://flybitlux.com/how-many-commercial-planes-crash-a-year.

"Mom, I think pandas are one of my favorite animals," she declared. "Or maybe a turtle, since Clide lives at our house."

"Yeah, I'm a big fan of them, too," I said.

"What's your favorite animal?" she asked.

Since I could remember, my favorite animal had always been a white tiger. I wasn't sure why, but there was something about their strength and beauty all rolled into one creature that I'd long admired and felt deeply connected to. Recalling its beauty and strength made me think a little more about this connection between tigers and fear that Dr. Temple and I had just been talking about.

Ironically, when I pictured my fears as imaginary tigers, they were the orange tigers, ferocious and loud, chasing their zebra victim. I had felt much like the running zebra for years now, avoiding orange tigers at all costs. I realized I had some work to do in shifting my perspective, and I decided to use Sapolsky's story as a catalyst for change.

In my mind's eye, I combined the fierce orange tiger and the peacefully grazing black-and-white-striped zebra into one beautiful, brave white tiger—both predator and prey, ferocious and gentle. This tiger I could sit with and allow its presence to fuel my courage instead of just wishing it would go away. In doing so, I began to feel more empowered and at peace. I would often imagine the animal beside me, a companion who was fiercely protecting me *and* encouraging me to step farther out toward the pasture, to graze and drink with more presence while still alert. Fear would accompany me but no longer call the shots.

When I first started cognitive behavioral therapy (CBT)[3] with Dr. Temple, I noticed subtle changes in my thinking right away. CBT is a type of therapy often used for anxiety, depression, and OCD that focuses on thinking (cognition), action (behavior), and ways to evaluate and modify

---

3 Institute for Quality and Efficiency in Health Care, *In Brief: Cognitive Behavioral Therapy (CBT)* (InformedHealth, 2022), https://www.ncbi.nlm.nih.gov/books/NBK279297.

both. Cognition and action are ultimately tied to how one feels, though as I would learn, emotions are the most fleeting and unreliable piece of the puzzle. It's not that we should discount their importance; rather, emotions should not be the only things that we use to choose our actions. The work wasn't easy, though, and it continues. Every day is a process of becoming more mindful and reframing thoughts.

As with making changes to any habit, mindset, or addiction, the first step is awareness. Let me be clear: I've always been aware of my thoughts—especially the loud inner critic ones—but I'm talking about the kind of mindful awareness in which you take notice and then let the thoughts pass through you or express them without shame or attachment. It's not an easy task, but it's a practice worth investigating.

My continued CBT sessions with Dr. Temple stretched me in ways that triggered rebellion, avoidance, and helplessness. One key component to panic and OCD therapies is known as exposure and response prevention (ERP),[4] or exposure therapy for short. Along with CBT, exposure therapy puts you in the direct path of thoughts, objects, or experiences that trigger fear so that, with the care and guidance of a practitioner and a plan, you can essentially retrain your brain to lessen the intensity of fear, as well as reduce avoidant behaviors and safety behaviors.

To break it down, safety behaviors are the actions, such as excessive handwashing or checking and rechecking appliances, that create an (often false) sense of security. People with OCD are often compelled to create rituals that, if not performed after being triggered or if interrupted, can lead to even more panic and anxiety. Once these rituals are completed, there is a sense of relief. Avoidant behaviors can vary, but it's usually making any kind of choice to avoid the trigger in the first place, such as deciding not to eat at a potluck because then I can avoid the stress of worrying about whether

---

4   "Exposure and Response Prevention (ERP)," International OCD Foundation, accessed
      December 19, 2024, https://iocdf.org/about-ocd/treatment/erp.

or not my food is contaminated, or going completely out of my way on a drive to avoid having to cross a bridge that causes me to feel panic.

When Dr. Temple and I first started with ERP, I was *highly* resistant (which, as it turns out, is a pretty normal response). I first had to decide what phobia or exposure I was willing to tackle, and this is when I learned how important it was to weigh benefits and risks in real-life scenarios to give concrete meaning and reward to the work of ERP. I had decided to prioritize my fear of heights, and we are talking just the second story here—not six, twelve, or twenty flights up. At the time, my bonus daughter, Bella, was swimming competitively, and I'd not been able to sit with her brother, Tobey, and the rest of the family at her last meet because they were all sitting in the second-tier balcony of the pool by the time I'd gotten there. Instead, I walked to the lower level and stood by the door, embarrassed and alone.

I decided that it would be well worth it to start working on becoming more comfortable with sitting in the balcony so that I could come to the next swim meet, have a better view, and cheer her on without my own internal drama. Dr. Temple and I set up a plan in our session that I would execute during the week: I was to head to the downtown mall during my lunch break, take the escalator to the second floor, and walk a lap. It might sound easy enough, but I couldn't do it. The first time I went to the mall, I took two wobbly steps off the top of the escalator and froze. I took a couple ragged breaths as other people coming off the escalator walked around me. My knees buckled, and I wanted to drop to the floor. Instead, I turned, reached out awkwardly for the railing of the down escalator, and willed my feet forward onto its first step. As I descended, I felt defeated and wiped away tears.

I tried again the next day, this time with the help of a coworker who agreed to go on this odd quest with me. We got to the top of the escalator, and I paused again. "I need your arm," I said as I reached out, my hand flailing a bit, and hooked my arm in hers. We walked the lap. I closed my eyes at times, remembering to slow my breath rather than hold it. My legs were weak but still moving. I felt more triumphant, even if I was clutching another human for safety from a fall that would never happen.

During my next session, Dr. Temple encouraged me to try it again, but alone. He spoke more about safety behaviors and how they can slow or halt the results of exposure therapy. I reluctantly agreed, but as I parked for my session the following week—having not returned to the mall at all—I became frustrated and angry. I was going to defend my avoidance of the exposure therapy and say that I just didn't have the time. But the reality was I wanted to give up. I just didn't feel like I could tackle this exposure homework alone. It felt too heavy, nearly impossible, and as I got out of the car, I began to wonder whether any of this was going to work.

I started walking across the second-story bridge that connects the parking ramp to the hospital—one that I had managed to walk solo at least three times by now. It was short, usually full of people, and pretty wide though surrounded by glass windows so I could see the street beneath me.

About ten steps in, I got stuck. My legs felt like lead, the floor beneath me began to disappear, and I faltered. I couldn't continue the fifteen or so steps across into the main hall of the hospital. Ahead of me, three men were working on some electrical wires in the ceiling, and others were walking behind me and toward me. I became acutely aware of the other people on the bridge. I worried that they would think I was rude or crazy standing there in the middle of this thoroughfare, so I took out my phone and held it to my ear, pretending like I was standing there for a reason.

I wanted to call my doctor, whose office was just a few feet away, and tell him to come rescue me because I was so scared of turning around and failing but too terrified to take another step forward. I didn't want to quit. I didn't want to turn around and go back and feel like I'd lost all that I'd been working toward. But as the time passed, the anxiety intensified. Vertigo set in more heavily, and I could no longer hold back my tears. To top it off, I was now late for my appointment.

Defeated, I turned back toward the parking ramp, hurrying down and around the cars to the ground-level sidewalk. I headed over to the main entrance of the hospital and gathered myself back together as I hurried down the hall, into the elevator, and out on the second floor in front of Dr. Temple's office on the other side of the bridge.

"Well, that was a failure," I scoffed, feeling embarrassed and angry at myself.

"You made it here, didn't you?" Dr. Temple met me with more compassion than I'd given myself.

"Yes, but I couldn't do it. I got stuck, avoided the bridge, and then was totally late for the appointment," I said with frustration.

"Those are all true," Dr. Temple replied, "and what would you like to do differently next time?"

I shook my head, not knowing what would even be possible. "Everything just feels impossible," I said, despondent.

Dr. Temple empathized and asked if I needed to slow it down or change it up. "Am I pushing you too hard?" he asked.

I sheepishly told him no, and though I felt weak, I agreed to hit the hospital bridge again: this time, he and I together.

He walked me out toward the bridge and stood nearby as I laughed nervously and looked around. I took a couple steps, as feeble as a ten-month-old. My face was now flushed, and my eyes darted around at the others walking by.

Dr. Temple spoke a reminder: "These other people don't care what you're doing."

"Ugh, this is embarrassing," I breathed, not wanting to take another step.

"They are all off in their own worlds, thinking about their own problems," he noted. His hands gently folded at his waist, his enduring patience palpable.

"This isn't fair," I grumbled in his direction.

He walked toward me. "How about I walk in front of you? One step at a time?" he offered. We started along that way—until midway through, I got stuck, and he kept going. My knees began to buckle.

"I can't do this," I whispered, hunching over and placing my hands on my knees. He came back and offered me his arm, which I batted away—determined not to use a physical crutch, though not ready to give up the mental safety of his nearby presence.

He stopped just a beat in front of me and waited. I took a step toward him, then another, until we had both made it across.

He smiled at me. "Good. Now let's go back," he said. He turned and took two steps ahead, then another, and I followed close behind. I walked taller and moved a little faster until we reached the hospital entrance once more.

"This time, just you," he instructed. We took a breath together, and I looked at him, his eyes kind and encouraging. He held his arm up and gestured toward the parking ramp.

I moved forward a few steps, then darted quickly across so I didn't lose momentum. Safely on the other side, I turned and looked at Dr. Temple across the bridge.

He smiled. I pumped my hands up and down, triumphant.

"See you next week!" he called out with a wave.

"Yes! Thank you!" I waved back, filled with a new sense of pride at what I'd just accomplished. I turned on my heels and bounced toward my car.

I was learning that it was all a process. One failure didn't have to mean that it was time to just quit. Some days, I could walk the bridge; other days, I couldn't. But what I stopped doing was making myself wrong on the days when the anxiety was too much to bear. I realized that fear doesn't just disappear, that it ebbs and flows not only in presence but also in intensity. It was a vital piece of understanding for continuing the work.

Ongoing exposure work during that time, however, became increasingly difficult. The more exposures that Dr. Temple wanted me to confront, the more I became resistant. The parts of me that wanted to ensure my safety at all costs didn't want to play this game anymore. The status quo was safer, even if it made me miserable. I was feeling so alone in the work, and the practices started to feel impossible. I didn't understand how I could get out of this deep, dark hole of overwhelm and exhaustion without someone just pulling me out and doing the work for me. Where was my magic wand? Why couldn't I just snap my fingers and be done with this?

I started canceling my appointments and refusing to do exposure work, until finally, my resistance left us at a standstill. If I wasn't willing or ready to tackle anything more complex than a second-story bridge, then why was I even in Dr. Temple's office?

The orange tiger had won. I stopped going to therapy sessions altogether. I resigned myself to a future in which I would never get on an airplane. I would continue to be a disappointment to Andrew, who would just keep traveling without me. We would live these separate lives, and I would fall further down the well of despair—feeling like I couldn't measure up against an impossible reality. I was pulled away from my foundational beliefs of hope, possibility, and connection. I was drowning in a sea of disappointment in myself; the weight of responsibility and the ongoing torture of fear seemed to be doing everything to prevent me from seeing a way through.

The work I had done with Dr. Temple wasn't futile, though. Even if I couldn't continue to walk bridges or tackle bigger exposures at the time, I'd learned some really valuable lessons that would sustain me until I returned to his office a couple years later to start again. Regardless of being resistant to the process of exposure therapy, I had a new understanding of the role fear played in my life. I understood it to be temporary; I understood that I had to allow it to be there instead of just wishing it would go away. I had to celebrate the small wins every step of the way and forgive myself for the times when I felt I had no choice but to let fear win and avoid whatever might be triggering in the moment.

Brave Reflection

Sometimes the work is more complex than we imagine. We can't tie these experiences neatly in a bow and close them off. There is an ebb and flow to healing work, and it's imperative to be compassionate with yourself through it. It is okay to not be okay. Some days, your bravery looks like just getting by. Other days, it looks triumphant. Embracing the tiger means that we can love ourselves at each point along the way.

Here, the invitation is to reflect on your relationship with fear, anxiety, and self-doubt. As you consider the following questions, remember that it is important to hold on to hope and that each moment is a new beginning, and remember that you are cultivating resilience every step of the way:

- What is your relationship to fear, and do you want to embrace it in a new way?
- How can you celebrate the small steps along your own journey?
- How can you keep going, even when it's hard, and try again tomorrow?

If you are sharing your self-discoveries on social media, use #EveryDayImBrave, and let us know how you are celebrating your bravery and cultivating more compassion for yourself and others on the path. You can also go to www.everydayimbrave.com to support you with additional resources.

8

PURPOSE WORK

AS I NEARED MY THIRTY-NINTH BIRTHDAY, I realized something was truly amiss. The weeks leading up to the day were desolate and hard. For the first time maybe ever, I didn't want to celebrate; I didn't want to acknowledge my birthday at all. I wasn't afraid of being older. I just wanted to skip it—to not pay any attention to the milestone—or, more aptly, to myself.

What I really wanted was to disappear. I wanted to escape the seemingly never-ending dirge and replace it with a life that felt free, joyous, connected, and purposeful—a life that just didn't seem possible. I managed to get through the days, mustering every ounce of energy I had to get out of bed with just enough time to get the kids off to school and land at work. I barely showered, suffering debilitating vertigo and panic every time I stepped in it. I washed as fast as I could, sometimes even sitting on the floor of the tub because I worried that I'd fall and crack my head on the tile or the water spout and be left alone to die.

Depression came on slowly in the months leading up to my wedding with Andrew, but it would be nearly a year later before I'd recognize how deeply I was suffering and that I really needed help. I was fatigued, eating cupcakes and chips for solace and gaining weight. I had headaches a few times a week and became nervous whenever I had to leave my house much outside of the routine of school, work, kids' activities, and Sunday dinner at my folks' house. Even grocery shopping became difficult: I'd push the cart down the aisle and feel like the rows of cereal and canned goods were caving in on me. The even floor felt angled, slanted, unstill. I'd shuffle through urgently, willing it to be over.

When I heard myself telling people at work that I wasn't having a birthday this year and letting my family know that it would be better to just skip any traditional dinner celebration, that tipped me off. So did knowing that Andrew and I weren't connecting very much. I had shut down in so many ways, and his frustration mixed with his fear about my yearning to disappear prompted me to pick up the phone and make an appointment with Dr. Temple.

It was hard getting back on the horse, so to speak, having been about two years since I'd last talked with Dr. Temple. I was a little ashamed to have quit, but he acknowledged the bravery and resilience it took to come back. In my desolation, I didn't feel that I had much purpose for being on the planet, but the purpose work ahead with Dr. Temple would reignite my passion for helping not only myself but others who were struggling too.

When I arrived and we got through formalities, he asked me how I saw myself. "Stuck in a cage without a lock," I told him, and I envisioned this cage as being deep inside my belly. I was a locked soul, desperately wanting out—weak and beaten, with no clear path ahead. I felt utterly hopeless. It was time to wake up again, out of the darkness, and peer into the world anew, and I knew I needed Dr. Temple's help to do it.

He and I also had a conversation about my resistance to doing the exposure work. He acknowledged that he had learned a few things from me, and I appreciated knowing that even as a challenging patient, I had provided him with a gift in the exchange. When we had stopped working together, I was deflated and frustrated. I didn't feel that I could continue to do the work on my own. I couldn't face these exposures alone, and that's what he had been asking me to do.

"Safety behaviors can be people too," he had said. But I was already feeling so alone, and doing more work on my own, even for myself, just felt impossible. He now understood and reflected that maybe he had pushed a little too hard, too fast, and that this time, we would start small.

And so we did.

Dr. Temple handed me a worksheet in that first meeting after I returned. At the top, it said something like, "Unfurling of Hands," and it was an exercise in both relaxation and allowing, in transforming resistance and walls into openness and possibility. I first had to feel even a glimmer of hope that change was possible.

And so my homework was to sit or stand and notice my hands. If my fists were clenched, I was to unfurl them. And even if I was neutral, I was to practice holding them open and facing upward or outward in a pose of receiving. It was simple, but it wasn't always easy. It was a vulnerable practice, and I came back the next week with a mix of cynicism and hope. When he handed me the next worksheet that was about the practice of smiling, I may have rolled my eyes.

And yet this was where I truly needed to begin.

So for a few weeks, I practiced holding open my palms and turning up the corners of my mouth. I resisted, scoffed, and then kind of giggled at myself when I began to notice a subtle shift. It became easier to do, more natural even. I'd smile for real more often than I had in months, and it didn't feel like work. If you've ever experienced depression, you know how much energy and muscle strength it actually takes to smile when you walk by a coworker in the hallway or have to make small talk with the checkout clerk. It can be a real challenge to summon the mask that covers the numbness, anger, sadness, and fear.

This subtle shift also allowed me to return to the mentors and teachings I'd relied on previously and perceive them in a new way, as well as to be guided toward new mentors who taught me about chakra energy systems and the universal laws of physics. Each of these experiences helped me avoid feeling deeply overwhelmed and negative while I dreamed up what the next iteration of my life might look like with more clarity and wisdom.

The kids were growing and becoming more independent before my eyes, and that shifted my energy reserves as well. While managing the household and all the activities was still challenging, I'd have these little pockets of time when someone wasn't urgently needing me. Most often, these were spent in the car, or on the sidelines, or in the dance studio lobby awaiting the end of a class or lesson, but they were moments when I got to choose what I thought about, what I read, who I texted, and what I listened to.

So I chose books and podcasts that helped me understand how intentionality, discipline, and energy worked to propel me forward in a new and more self-compassionate direction. I spent time writing and crafting a potential entrepreneurial vision in which I could balance my creative work with education and motivation. I was even able to return to performing—something I hadn't done since high school—taking on roles in our local community theatre that allowed me to sing, dance, and connect with others on the stage to bring stories to life. Those moments were my lifeline.

One afternoon, on a particularly good day, Dr. Temple and I had a simple yet mind-blowing conversation that would change everything for me moving forward. We were talking about starting some exposure work again now that the thought-reframing work of CBT had helped pull me out of the dark.

"Dr. Temple, when I feel this good, I feel like I have the strength and energy to get on an airplane or take the glass elevator to the fourth floor. But when I'm feeling low, sad, and defeated—doing that kind of work feels absolutely impossible," I admitted.

"Well, what if you did it *regardless* of how you feel?" he responded.

"Oh," is all I could reply. I was quiet for a moment.

"What if you just let the feeling be there and take the next step anyway?" Dr. Temple proposed. He was often telling me to just *let the feeling be there.* I'd imagine a little cloud of fear atop my shoulder, pulling it out of my head and putting it over to the side, just allowing this little fluffy gray cloud over there coming along for the ride. It was not unlike the white tiger that I also imagined sitting next to me, tall and strong.

"*Regardless* of how I feel?" I repeated back to him.

"Yes," he said.

For a long, long time, I thought that feelings were the most important part of this life experience because, for me at least, emotions and feelings in the body were the absolute most potent and intense component. It didn't make sense to me to go against what I was feeling, which is where a lot of my resistance came from: *How dare he ask me to walk that bridge! Doesn't he know I feel scared?*

But what Dr. Temple was pointing to wasn't devaluing my emotions. On the contrary, suggesting that I allow the feeling to be present was actually an acknowledgment of its voice. I was the one fighting with fear all the time, angry that it was present, wishing for it to go away instead of listening to the part of me that needed to express and experience the fear. What was most important was that acknowledgment, surrendering to its existence so that I could stop fighting and make choices about actions and behaviors from a more neutral place.

"So, you're saying . . . it doesn't matter how I feel, to just do the thing anyway," I said, pushing against him a little bit with my language.

He smiled. "Not that it doesn't matter," he corrected, "but that your wise mind—the part of you that is the observer—can notice, accept, and decide what to do rather than just letting fear, or your emotional mind, call all the shots. It's often called *opposite action.*"

"Opposite action?" I asked.

"Yes," Dr. Temple explained, "like when you don't feel like getting out of bed, but your wise, observer mind knows that it's better for you to get up and start your day instead of continuously hitting the snooze button and then ending up late for work."

"Hey, I resemble that remark," I chuckled.

Dr. Temple laughed a little. "But seriously," he continued, "opposite action is a vital piece of this work. You aren't going to feel good all the time. Feelings are like the weather: They ebb and flow. But your actions—your commitment to feeling the fear and doing it anyway—that's where the change happens."

"What if I did it *regardless* of how I feel?" The repetition out of my mouth was helping me integrate the thought. It seemed like such a novel idea, and I began to see even more how much anxiety had been making my decisions for me every single day. Unlike the zebra who returned again and again to the watering hole, I was canceling lunch dates with friends because I'd suddenly feel sick, scared that I'd not be able to eat or know what to talk about. I'd not applied for a promotion because it would have required me to travel a few days out of the year. I had avoided the concert I wanted to see just because the only seats available were in the balcony.

I began applying this simple principle of "regardless" to multiple areas of my life, not just exposure work. I would look into the future and think about where I wanted to be in my career, in my relationships, in my creative work, and I began to develop a writing practice, writing even when I didn't *feel* like it. I got out of bed when the alarm went off even if I didn't *feel* like it. I showed up for my friends, my kids, and my work even if I didn't *feel* like it, and I marveled at how good I actually began feeling in the middle of doing the thing I didn't feel like doing.

You see, when you can view the bigger picture; have a desired plan for what you want life to look like; and acknowledge the fear, inertia, boredom, and dread to come along for the ride, the feeling eventually shifts. There is less resistance, or at least it shows up a lot less often, and the momentum of one step at a time toward your vision changes your life over time.

It's not magic. In fact, it often feels like work. But it *is* magical.

The work can come in tiny steps toward reshaping how we feel from the inside out. Sometimes, as is the case with the unfurling of hands and smiling, it has to come from the outside in. We have to believe we can become the version of ourselves that we want to see out in the world, and often, that starts out by doing the thing even when we don't feel like it.

When depression or prolonged sadness looms large, it's important to talk with your therapist about what types of activities might help you start feeling better. In CBT, choosing to take action (e.g., getting out of bed when you don't feel like it or turning on some happy music even if you'd rather listen to the saddest song in the world) will often shift your mood. It's called behavior activation,[1] and it's been shown to help over time. But note: It *does* take time.

The white tiger continued to walk with me through this process—so much so that I couldn't resist buying a giant white tiger stuffed animal that I saw in a toy shop window one fall afternoon. It rode with me on a solo car trip for a writing retreat in Wisconsin, resting in my lap as a comforting pet while I breathed over bridges and took courage along for the ride. It continues to sit with me to this day, finding a home in my office as I write.

Sometimes, the white tiger would roar warnings that didn't always hold merit; other times, it would rest at my feet—content and quiet. When I faltered on a bridge, avoided an elevator, or canceled a date with a friend, I didn't punish the parts of me that were afraid, and the next time, I'd call on the majestic white tiger to help me summon the courage I'd need to show up to do the work.

---

1   Albert Bonfil and Suraji Wagage, "Part 8: Opposite Action, Behavioral Activation, and Exposure," in *A Course in CBT Techniques: A Free Online CBT Workbook* (Cognitive Behavioral Therapy Los Angeles), https://cogbtherapy.com/opposite-action-behavioral-activation-and-exposure.

Brave Reflection

We can reflect on what it means to continue to do the brave purpose work as life's challenges ebb and flow. Let's take some time to create a list of things you could do that will help you move toward a more positive state of mind. Maybe it's a card game with a friend or your kid, maybe it's taking a walk around the block, or maybe it's simply enjoying a cup of coffee on the front porch and listening to the tree leaves rustle in the wind. Whatever it is, think simple and small—something that you could muster up just enough energy to do, even and especially when you don't *feel* like doing anything at all. When you are feeling down or like the weight of the world is on your shoulders, return to this list.

- Step one: Create a list of activities or actions you can take when you're feeling down and want to shift your energy or perspective.
- Step two: Post that list somewhere you can easily return to it.
- Step three: Choose one thing to do today, and take that brave opposite action into the next moment.

Once complete, share your list on social media and use #EveryDayImBrave so that others can get inspired to create their own lists. You can find some examples and additional resources at www.everydayimbrave.com.

9

CROSSCURRENTS

I SAT IN DR. TEMPLE'S OFFICE in quiet resolve. It was early April, just after my fortieth birthday party that I had celebrated jointly with my then-eighteen-year-old daughter. We had put together a musical theatre–themed karaoke extravaganza and invited our friends and family to dress as their favorite characters. My parents arrived in '70s garb, my mom in a long blond wig over her short silver hair and sporting round sunglasses, my dad with a giant peace sign necklace and a butterfly collar. One of their favorite Broadway shows they saw live was *Hair*, and they wore it well.

I was dressed as a 1920s-era flapper girl, a nod to *Chicago the Musical*, and Andrew wore a zoot suit to match. The room was filled with music and mayhem, and as Shelby and I got up to thank the guests for coming and playing along, the song "Helpless" from the musical *Hamilton* began to play. Shelby turned to me and started singing a parody version about our lives, and when different members of the crowd joined in and began a ballroom dance routine, I instantly knew I'd been flash-mobbed!

Andrew even sang a verse he'd prepared about the love and family we'd been sharing for the last six years, and there wasn't a dry eye in the room. It was truly one of the best gifts I'd ever received.

But it was tainted by the knowing in my heart. As we celebrated that night, it was hard for me to put aside the resentment I'd been feeling in my second marriage. Because Andrew traveled so much for work and was gone for weeks and sometimes months at a time, I'd felt quite unsupported, dismissed, and lonely, though I was too busy spinning all the plates to even know what it was I truly needed and speak to it directly. Things had been messy for quite some time, and as I came out from under depression's hold, I felt that I was once again at a crossroads.

I was set to leave my corporate job a few weeks later since Andrew had found stable work through a company whose headquarters were in DC, and I planned to return to the classroom part-time and work on my writing. Nick had also moved back to the area, so I had a little more help with the kids on a regular basis. There were positive changes coming, and I thought I could be patient and wait out this rough patch.

But a little voice inside me kept whispering, *For what?*

Dr. Temple looked at me. We had been working through the innards of my relationship since I'd returned to therapy a year earlier. In addition to the CBT and exposure work, we talked in detail about my marriage. Together, we parsed what was mine to work on, understanding the challenges of what it's like for others to live with my OCD symptoms, such as the constant questioning and reassurance about how things were cooked or washed, or refusing to eat foods that were on the okay-to-eat list just because I couldn't let go of an intrusive thought that it was somehow no longer safe.

I wanted to stick it out because I didn't want to be that person who got divorced a second time. I didn't want to disappoint my parents again. I didn't want to break up our family home, our five kids having grown up together for years. I worried most about them; their bond was precious. I'd been hanging on, hoping something would change, but fear was present here too, and I no longer wanted to make my decisions with fear at the helm.

So as I sat there, recounting with mixed emotions the previous weekend's celebration, I simply couldn't unknow the knowing. I was done.

"Crosscurrents," Dr. Temple said to me.

"What?" I responded, unsure where this was going.

"Crosscurrents," he repeated, "in the water." His wisdom didn't just come from years of psychoanalytic and behavioral health research. He'd done his own work. "We come across them often, these moments when it can feel like we are being pulled in multiple directions at once." I nodded as he went on, "Ultimately, we have to look at these currents from an eagle-eye perspective, we have to see the bigger picture, and then sometimes, we just have to surrender and let the water reveal the direction we are meant to go."

I left Dr. Temple's office with a little bit of clarity—and a sinking feeling. I decided to stop by the river on my way home to journal a bit before returning to the hustle and bustle of carpool, dinner, and kid activities.

There is a walking bridge in town by the University of Iowa's student union that connects the campus to the other side of the river. It had always been a favorite place of mine. I had good memories from my teen years there, and I even drew a picture of it once and probably still have it in some box. I walked to and fro on the bridge and then decided to sit closer to the riverbank. As I settled in on the concrete edge and began to watch the movement of the water, I saw clearly the crosscurrents that flowed along.

My eyes followed the pathway of a small branch downstream as it spun into a new current that took it diagonally off its path. I watched a pair of dragonflies touch down to skim the muddy waters and noticed the concentric circles they created, shifting and spiraling the flow at different points along the river.

If we spend some time taking in nature, we can see how it often reflects back to us what we are seeking. I looked at the ripples in the water, the fish underneath seemingly unphased by the drifts. They swam with intention, yes, but also with flow. This is the balance I continued to seek: how to live intentionally, consciously, and with purpose while also surrendering to what is out of my control. I wanted to allow the magic of nature, of the universe, of my own intuition and inner knowing to guide me despite how difficult the choices became.

I knew then what I had to do, and when Andrew returned from his latest month-long work trip to the little island of Vanuatu, we had a heartbreaking conversation and made a plan.

In some ways, I felt like a complete failure. Here I was again: divorce, job change, and, this time, the added stress of selling a home I dearly loved because there was no way I could afford it on my own. What was supposed to be a time of exploration and freedom after leaving my corporate job became a mad scramble for additional work just to get by.

The result was a little full circle. I had left my teaching job in 2007 but had returned to the exact same school in the exact same role that I'd left—working with struggling adolescent readers, the kids who forever have a place in my heart. I had been hired to work only half-time, which had been all I needed, but now that Andrew and I were separated and selling the house, I wasn't going to have any of his financial support to spend the other half of my days writing and taking care of the kids like I'd hoped.

So I applied for as many other part-time jobs that I could and even interviewed for the same position I'd just left in corporate education, but in a different department. The last thing I wanted to do was return to that work, but even at half-time, it would pay me more than my current teaching salary. I was immediately offered the job, and I told them I had to think about it.

I called my friend Shanti to help talk me through the decision. She not only knew firsthand the struggle of working this kind of job, but she wouldn't bullshit me either.

"Renee, listen," she said to me on the phone while I paced back and forth in the school parking lot before the first day of school. "You took yourself and ran from that place. Don't go back."

"I know," I said. "You're right. You're right . . . but the money is good, and maybe it will just be temp—"

She cut me off: "The money isn't worth it. And we all know it's no half-time job. The deadlines alone will feel like full-time, and your attention would be split. With teaching, which is also a full-on experience, it will feel like *two* full-time jobs."

"You're right. You're right," I sighed.

"Just think about it," she encouraged me. "Something will come. There will be a way through."

At this point, I'd been living back in my parents' basement for a few weeks with my two youngest kids (Shelby was now in a college dorm down the street—her things in diaspora between my parents' house, the dorm, and the storage shed I rented for my furniture and anything else I didn't need to bring with me to my parents' home). I was desperate to get my finances in order enough to start looking for a new place for us to land.

"You're right," I told Shanti. "It will." My phone vibrated. "I gotta run. The counseling office is calling me on the other line. I better go in the building. Thank you, Shanti. I don't know where I'd be without you sometimes. Truly. Love you!"

"Love you too, girl," she responded. "It's all gonna work out."

I hung up the phone and headed into the back door of the school building and straight to the counseling office. Miranda was sitting in her office. The door was open, and she waved me in.

"Close the door," she said. I did as I was told. The bustle of the kids in the hallway muted, and I sat down. "Did Nicole call you yet?" she asked. Nicole was our assistant principal. I shook my head no and suddenly worried that I was being cut entirely or something else horrifying was about to happen.

"Okay, well, I guess I can just ask you," Miranda continued. "We had a change in staffing. It's not finalized yet, but one of our other literacy teachers is taking a part-time position as an instructional coach, and we need someone to take over her morning classes . . . starting tomorrow."

Miranda's voice faded into the background, and my brain buzzed. *This is the way*, I thought. *I'll have* one *job. I'll have a full-time salary, and I'll be on the kids' schedule, so it will be a little more feasible to still manage the evening activities and such. I'll have the means to find a house. Do I want to work full-time? No. Do I need to work full-time? Yes.*

I refocused on Miranda's voice. "So I know you were hired part-time, and that was what you wanted," she was saying, "but is there any way you would consider being full-time and take these classes?"

I smiled. "Absolutely," I replied.

And that was that. I didn't have to run back to the soul-sucking corporate cubicle job. Instead, I got to run toward a little more freedom, and the way through the darkness continued to open up, bit by bit, as I faced the challenges ahead.

In quiet moments, I'd often ask myself, *How did I get here again? Am I ever going to be able to maintain some sense of stability in my life? Am I ever going to have the time and space to create more ease in my life and follow my creative pursuits? Am I scarring my kids forever? Why does money have to control everything in our lives? If I could just focus on my kids, my writing, and my heart's work, then everything would be fine.*

While I was confident in my choices, it still wasn't an easy transition for anyone. It was raw and humbling, and at times, I felt ashamed and broken for having to seemingly start all over again.

By Thanksgiving that year, the kids and I settled into a beautiful condo nestled next to a park and biking trail. We began anew and just kept moving forward. Time doesn't stop, and neither do life's experiences, so I had to show my kids what resilience looks like.

Staying stuck in the cycle of shame wasn't serving me, or anyone else for that matter. So I had to look at *why* I was back here and reflect on the lessons I needed to learn this time around that I wasn't leaning into the first time I'd gone through this massive transition and awakening.

First, I knew I had to slow down—slow down my actions, my thoughts, and my impulses. And I had to take a good hard look at how much of a role my fears and need for control played in the destruction of my relationship; I had to do my own inner work if I was ever going to see some outer change. Relationships are mirrors for us. The learning comes not when we give away our power to the other but when we can recognize our part and take full responsibility for the choices we make, whether it's the choice to stay silent when things upset us so that we don't rock the boat or deciding that there is only one way to slice up a marriage into bits. So I devoted the next few years to limited focal points: my teaching job, my kids' needs, continued therapy and self-reflection, and a new partner who understood and also needed the same kind of spaciousness I'd yearned for, like the one between Khalil Gibran's pillars of marriage.

And it went like that for a couple of years. I had my space, my kids grew and thrived, and I continued to work with Dr. Temple on allowing fear to come along for the ride. One day, we were mulling over the latest panic episode I'd had at school, which included a full tachycardia episode that left me racing to the teachers' lounge to pull ice packs out of the freezer and sit with them on my face and chest in order to bring my heart back to a normal rhythm.

Dr. Temple asked me, "How do you know that you can handle panic feelings?"

I wondered whether this was a trick question. "Because I do all the time," I scoffed.

I thought I was just being a smart-ass, but this wise man sat in front of me, silent for a moment longer so that what I had just said could echo in my mind.

Because I do all the time.

"Huh," I nodded. "That's it, isn't it? I know I can handle feelings of panic because I literally survive them *all* the time!"

He smiled, that twinkle in his eye beaming with pride.

"Huh," I said, taking another breath and letting it sink in while he turned back to his desk, pen in hand, and scribbled the words I'd just said on the bottom of his legal pad. He tore it off and handed it to me. I read it aloud:

"I can handle panic feelings because I do all the time."

This flip in perspective from *I panic all the time; therefore, I'm out of control, and I never know when it's gonna hit* to *I can handle feelings of panic because I do all the time* suddenly became a newfound source of strength. This was a new knowing, an assurance that I can and will continue to handle the feelings of panic that creep up often because I've proven to myself, over and over again, that I can.

Is panic fun? No.

Can I survive it? Yes.

I was moving from a mindset of *I'm damaged because I panic all the time* to *I'm resilient because I panic all the time and survive.* This new perspective gave me more strength and courage. It also lessened the added pressure, fear, and shame that can come with panic attacks. Much like the crosscurrents in the water, this shift allowed me to lean further into the idea that panic symptoms will ease and change and that I'm strong enough to handle them. The ripples in the water and the cycles of life's challenges actually become an opportunity to expand our learning, growth, and resilience. We are better able to bounce back after hardship when we've got more tools in our toolbox to help us move through the transitions, surrender to the new current, and, when the way clears, steer our boat in the direction we wish to go.

I took that little piece of paper from Dr. Temple home with me and attached it to a photo clip that had been sitting empty on the bookshelf in my bedroom. To this day, it remains in that clip, now proudly displayed in my office and revisited in times when I need to remember my inner strength.

Brave Reflection

Sometimes we have to start over, again and again, until we can really integrate and embody a lesson life is teaching us. As we cycle through the process, though, we can see from a higher, more experienced perspective.

This is part of the brave work—to accept where we are so that we can have a clear sense of where we want to go. This is also how we cultivate resilience. We continue to face the challenges of a diagnosis, a struggling relationship, or a job or circumstance that feels impossible to get out of, yet we can become more resilient at every turn. We can handle getting knocked down because we have gotten back up every single time before. That, my friend, is resilience. That is bravery.

Use the following journal prompts to reflect on how you have cultivated resilience:

- When I think of cycles of awakening, of the lessons I am still learning, I _____.

- Even though I sometimes still struggle with _____ _____ , I can have compassion for myself because _____.

- Some patterns I notice are _____ , and what I've already learned from them is _____ _____.

What patterns came up? What can you appreciate or celebrate about what you've learned? If you'd like to share your aha moments on social media, use #EveryDayImBrave to celebrate your continued evolution and resilience. There are also further resources available at www.everydayimbrave.com.

10

FLYING HIGH

I'VE ALWAYS THOUGHT THAT THE VIEW from an airplane was gorgeous: the rolling farmland across the Midwest, the setting sun sparkling across the horizon, the miniature cars making their way along the freeway. Flying made me nervous, but it didn't always scare me. In fact, the few flights I took as a teenager before the one that changed everything were undeniably easy: no tears, no drugs, and no hint of the sheer panic that was about to set in.

I was nineteen years old and had just completed my first year of college. My oldest brother, David, was getting married in Denver, Colorado, and the whole family was flying out to be a part of the mountaintop nuptials. We—my other brother, Eric; my parents; and I—flew from Detroit, and the three-hour flight into Denver International Airport was a piece of cake.

The ride home, however, was a different story. At the time, the Denver airport had a separate smoking lounge—pretty far from our boarding gate. Eric and I wanted to get a few last puffs of nicotine into our systems before takeoff and went off to find the elusive smoking lounge. In the mid-'90s, smoking was still kinda cool. My mom was especially frustrated with us, not only because we were smoking after she and my dad had quit fifteen years earlier to serve as a good example for us but also because that meant we would be leaving the bustling gate.

Assuring our parents that we had enough time to smoke and come back, we headed to the smoking lounge. On the way back to the terminal, we heard our names over the loudspeaker as a flight attendant called us to the gate. Our quick-paced walk turned into a sprint as we rounded the corner and saw my parents and a single flight attendant standing at the now-empty gate.

"Hurry up! They are going to leave without us!" my mother yelled, with undeniable fury in her voice.

"Shit!" I muttered to my brother and then yelled back to my mom, "Why did they board everyone early?!"

Winded and apologetic, we hurried down the ramp into the airplane and found our seats. I couldn't look at my mom, knowing I had disappointed and scared her. My heart, still pounding in my chest from the run and the nicotine, was pumping adrenaline through my veins fast.

I buckled myself into the window seat, my dad sat next to the aisle, and the seat between us remained empty. My mom and my brother sat in a similar formation in the row across from us. It was dusk, and I looked out the window and saw thunderclouds in the distance. Denver skies are known for rolling storms near the end of the day, the mountain air often unsteady.

I took some deep breaths to quiet the creeping restless feeling, and as the airplane began to pull away from the terminal, my imagination ran wild. I envisioned myself dashing from my seat, running down the aisle, and trying to deplane, knowing full well that they wouldn't let me through the doors. The fantasy repeated over and over in my head: In my mind's eye, I saw myself screaming and banging on the airplane door. The realization that there was no escape, no turning back, consumed me.

I was stuck. And I had no control over what was about to happen.

I leaned forward and looked across the aisle at my mom. "I think I need something, Mom," I said. She dug in her purse for the Xanax, broke one in half, and handed it down the line into my brother's hands, my father's hands, and finally, my own. I popped it in my mouth and took a quick drink of my Mountain Dew as we taxied across the runway and prepared to take off.

It is difficult to describe the sheer panic that shot through me as we picked up speed and lifted up off the ground. I felt myself falling, sinking deeper into the chair I clung to as we climbed higher into the sky. The plane shook as we passed through the thickening clouds, but once we were level, the shaking didn't cease. A storm began to rage, and the pilot came on the speaker to tell us we'd climb even higher to get above it, but as we did so, the plane would drop what felt like a hundred feet at a time.

I pulled my hooded sweatshirt off and buried my face in it knowing I was going to lose it. The Xanax, now fully operational in my system, released the fear into tears and muffled screams. My dad lifted the armrest between the middle seat and mine, and I fell to the side, curling up in fetal position, stuffing the sweatshirt farther into my mouth to dampen the sounds.

A flight attendant came by and asked if she could get me anything. I looked up at her, my eyes bloodshot as I gasped for air between sobs, and my dad merely turned her away and lay his arm across my back to try to soothe me.

For three hours, sinking and shaking from both the internal and external turmoil, I tried to gather myself together, to breathe more steadily, to speed time and diminish space until my feet hit the earth again.

When we finally descended into Detroit, I sat up and watched as the cars got bigger and bigger and we closed in nearer to the treetops. When the wheels touched the pavement, I gathered my things and dried my eyes. I was completely spent. My dad let me out into the aisle in front of him, and with a stronger resolve than I'd ever had about any decision before in my life, I turned to my family and said, "I am *never* doing that again."

And I didn't. Hell-bent and stubborn, I refused to believe I could ever get myself on a plane again. For more than twenty years, I missed weddings, funerals, and fun adventures with friends, all because the trips weren't drivable or I didn't have enough vacation days from work to plan for multiple days of driving. When asked about it, I'd merely tell people, "I don't fly."

Then, in 2017, I was faced with a decision I felt would make or break me. I'd been doing CBT and exposure work for a few years consecutively by then, and it had helped me to see the wisdom and benefit of facing some of the smaller everyday fears. But when my eldest brother, David, and his girlfriend, Chris, announced their engagement and their plans to have their wedding in January 2018 near their home in Florida, I didn't think I was up for this kind of challenge.

I fell into a tailspin trying to figure out how I was going to get my ass to Florida in the middle of winter without enough time off in the vacation bank to make the drive. As a teacher, I couldn't take a whole week off, especially not right after winter break. I just couldn't see a way through.

Back in Dr. Temple's office, I aired my frustrations.

"Why can't they get married in the summer?" I grumbled. "My brother is a teacher too. That's more time off for both of us, and then I don't have to take the kids out of school either."

"I'm hearing you say that this shorter window of availability makes it more challenging for you to drive to Florida for the wedding; is that right?" Dr. Temple asked.

"Exactly," I huffed, indignant in my position.

"Well, could you decide not to go?" His question hung in the air.

"I can't *not* show up," I said. "My brother would never forgive me!"

"You don't think he'd understand?" Dr. Temple asked.

"No, he would," I replied. "He'd be mad, but he'd get it. It's just . . . maybe that *I* wouldn't ever forgive myself."

"Ah, yes," Dr. Temple responded. "Being at his wedding is important to you?"

"Yes," I replied, and then I laughed because the rhetorical irony was just too good. "You know, the last flight I was ever on was returning from my brother's first wedding in Denver. If I managed to get myself on a plane again to go to his second wedding, well then, there's some kind of full-circle shit at play here."

He chuckled, "Yeah, that would be something, wouldn't it?"

And that became the story. For eight months, Dr. Temple and I worked regularly on the different steps it would take to move from "I'm never getting on a plane again" to actually executing a successful trip to Florida.

It was slow-moving. I first had to shift away from *never* to even considering the possibility that I might. We moved along the continuum of possibility and bravery until I was able to even say to other people that I was going to make it work—to book the flights, to walk through security and get on the plane.

We worked on my breath, talked through ways to distract my brain from intrusive and anxious thoughts, and took time to look at the evidence of how safe flying actually is. (People always *love* to tell me how much safer flying is than driving and then state statistics about car deaths. It's not really helpful, especially when interstate driving can *also* be really nerve-racking.) CBT is multifaceted and flexible in its approach, but the key is to reframe our thoughts and recognize the evidence in front of us. It's also about feeling prepared. For someone like me, with panic disorder, anxiety, and OCD, it's really helpful to have an idea of what to expect in a given situation.

As such, in the safety of the office, Dr. Temple took me through different visualization exercises of walking through the airport, getting on the plane and settling into my seat, and then enduring takeoff. Usually, that's as far as we could get before I'd have to pause, catch my breath, and remind myself that my feet were, in fact, on solid ground.

Dr. Temple and I also talked about medication. When I was a teenager, my mom would give me half a Xanax to fly sometimes, just to take the edge off. Now medication, too, was at the top of my do-not-consume list. The only thing I had been willing to take for years was Tylenol for headaches and Benadryl once in a great while, when absolutely needed. How was I going to reconcile the desire to take the edge off during flight with the fear of taking medication?

As winter descended upon us and I was closer and closer to making it to my brother's wedding, I began having in-depth chats with my boyfriend Ben, who happened to be a psychiatric nurse practitioner who routinely prescribed medication. He understood the nuances of different types of medications, their side effects, and the mechanics of how they worked. I also checked with my internal medicine doctor about the best options, and I agreed to work out a plan with Dr. Temple to try the medication in a safe environment first so I understood before the flight how I would react with it.

It's a bit of a joke how sensitive I am to medications and chemicals. We started, and I continue to this day, with the smallest dose of lorazepam (brand name Ativan) available: half a milligram. I also created safety behaviors and rituals that I still use today when I take medication. One ritual is that I have to make sure that someone else knows what I'm taking and when, just in case I have some sort of adverse reaction or something horrible happens to me and the emergency team needs to know what is in my bloodstream; these are the catastrophic thoughts that plague me. They either have to watch me take it, or I text them when I've taken it. The wiser part of my mind knows this is unnecessary, but OCD demands that I tell someone.

January arrived, and I felt as ready as I could be. Meditation music, medicine, my family, and my partner were all along for the ride. The morning of our flight to Florida, I couldn't eat and barely slept. I just kept moving, making sure that everything was in place for the dog sitter, checking that the kids' bags were accurately packed, checking and rechecking the departure times, and making sure everyone was ready to go.

When we arrived at the Eastern Iowa Airport and began unloading the car, I took a moment to breathe in the crisp cold air and looked up at the sky. I was grateful it was clear; the sky was bright blue, and the sun warmed the skin on my face even as my fingertips froze. I thanked Mother Nature for the perfect day and rolled my carry-on suitcase behind me as I followed the kids.

"Mom's doing it," Shelby whispered gleefully to Evan.

"I know!" he said, beaming back at her. Behind them, Lily slowed and stopped beside me, her own anxiety at peak levels. I reached my hand out, and she took it willingly. We squeezed our fingertips together a few times as we approached security. Ben turned back and did a head count. Once satisfied we were all present and accounted for, he turned back and handed the security guard his ID.

Going through security was chaotic but didn't take long. Once at our gate, I checked the time again. Ben and I decided that I'd take the medicine about thirty minutes before we boarded so that the effects would be fully in my system by takeoff. I walked over to the water fountain to refill my bottle and back over to the gate to find the kids nestled in the chairs, headphones on, bored and tired. I turned to Ben, checked the time again, and took a deep breath.

"Yeah," he said. "It's time."

I sat down, fished the pill bottle out of my backpack, and read the label no less than three times. I repeated the instructions over and over again in my mind, making sure I had the right medicine and the right dosage. I then unscrewed the cap and laid it face up on my leg and tipped the bottle gently so that a single tiny pill fell out and into the cap. I had to make sure my fingers didn't touch the pill because I hadn't just washed them.

I looked up at Ben. "It's okay," he assured me. "You can take it."

I looked back down at the pill, then around at my children, who were engaged in whatever was playing on their iPhones, and back up at Ben.

"Go ahead," he urged.

I picked up the bottle cap and held it in front of me. *You can do this,* I reassured myself. *You took it a week ago and were fine. You'll be just fine.* I took a deep breath and tipped the cap toward my open mouth and felt the pill land gently on my tongue. I resisted the urge to spit it out and breathed again before taking a big swig of water and swallowing. *No turning back.*

"There, it's done," I grumbled, and Ben smiled at me. I put the lid back on the bottle, drank a few more sips of water, and checked the time again. Each step of that morning's journey would be the same way: hesitation, breathing, surrendering.

You see, there is magic in surrender—that place of radical acceptance where you give up the fight and have no choice but to allow whatever will happen to happen. *Surrender* became a word I used to help me get closer to being able to trust the process and have a little faith that everything would be okay, despite the intrusive, catastrophic scenarios that would try to take hold of my mind. Focusing on surrender allows my muscles to relax, my mind to quiet, and a sense of freedom to arise.

I checked the time again and decided to head to the restroom once more so that I didn't have to use the facilities in the airplane. I was sitting in the stall when suddenly I noticed a funny sensation in my eyelids.

"Oh, there it is," I giggled to myself, feeling that familiar slight heaviness moving down from the top of my head, through my neck, and into my belly. I finished my business, stood, and wobbled a bit. "Whoop!" I giggled again. "Okay then, here we go."

I washed my hands and looked at myself in the mirror and smiled, impervious to the others around me. *I'm doin' it! Here we go! Whew!* I giggled again as I walked out, paying special attention to my feet beneath me to make sure I walked in a straight line. One foot, the next foot; another step, then another.

I slunk into my chair next to Lily and slid halfway down it. "Y'all, my eyeballs feel funny," I said.

"Mom's on drugs," Shelby snickered.

"I'm Flat Renee!" I announced. "You know, like Flat Stanley, from the books." I slid farther down the chair, my knees bent out in front of me, my back flat against the seat.

"Mom's high," Evan noted, the volume of his voice considerably louder than his sister's. We laughed when a few people looked in our direction, until the gate attendant interrupted with our first boarding announcement.

"Okay, familia! It is time," I said. As everyone around me started to gather their things, I walked over to the window and gazed at the Boeing 747, the sun reflecting off its front window. I rubbed my hands together, getting the energetic friction going, and stood firm, legs shoulder-width apart. I visualized tree roots extending out the soles of my feet, through the floor, and deep and wide into the earth below me. I took a deep breath and tilted my head upward, closing my eyes for a moment to feel the bright, sparkling sunlight beaming down on my face, through the top of my head, all through my body, and out my fingertips. I held my hands out toward the airplane, imagining a protective bubble of light surrounding it and all the people who would be aboard that day. And then, I offered up a silent prayer of gratitude.

Thank you for bringing me to this moment, I thought. *Thank you for the amazing, talented flight crew who are making this trip possible. Thank you for the health and well-being of me, my family, and everyone about to take flight. Thank you for the clear skies. Thank you for the brilliant minds that allow us to fly without wings of our own. Thank you for the opportunity to see my brother get married, for the sandy beach that my feet will soon be standing on, for the brilliant waters of the ocean shore that will welcome us.*

With tears in my eyes, I brought my hands to my heart, surrendering to the gratitude of the moment. I turned back to my family and smiled as they called our group number to board.

Shelby snapped pictures of me as I pulled my suitcase and danced my way down the ramp to release the jitters. "Mom's doin' it!" she said proudly.

We filed into the plane one by one. I smiled at the flight attendants, grateful for their calm presence, and took a peek at the pilots' control panel, grateful for their expertise. We made our way to row eight, where Ben and Evan helped us get our carry-ons into the overhead bins. The kids filed in to the left, Lily in the middle so both Evan and Shelby could help her navigate the nerves.

Ben sat in the aisle seat, and I took the middle. We took a few minutes to get situated, headphones out of my bag, meditation music at the right volume, pieces of gum passed around to help with the ear pressure during ascent. I looked down the aisle at my kids, blowing a kiss to each one of them.

"Everybody good down there?" I asked. Shelby and Evan gave me a thumbs-up.

Lily locked eyes with me. "Do you have your music on?" I asked. She nodded. "You're okay," I reassured her. She nodded again, and Evan took her right hand while Shelby cradled her left.

I took a deep breath and leaned back into my chair, turned the volume up on my phone, and wrapped my right arm around Ben's left elbow. He patted my knee, and I looked up at him. He smiled gently and whispered, "You've got this."

"Ladies and gentlemen, this is your captain speaking," said the disembodied voice over the speaker. I took one earbud out to listen in, watched as the flight attendants reviewed the safety features, and noticed the fear filling my throat.

Just allow it to be there, Dr. Temple's voice echoed in my mind.

I placed the earbud back in my ear as the flight attendants made one more pass down the aisle. As we began to taxi down the runway, my breath quickened, and my feet wanted to move, the impulse to escape starting in my toes. I took a slow conscious breath and rearranged my feet. I pulled my arm out of Ben's elbow and rubbed my thighs.

Just allow it to be there.

"Flight attendants, prepare for takeoff," directed the pilot. The aircraft picked up speed, and I felt my heart flutter. I took another slow breath, counting in for four and out for seven.

Surrender.

The nose of the plane lifted into the air, and I was pushed back into my seat. Tears flowed down my face, and I grabbed both armrests and held on, white-knuckled.

Surrender.

I unfurled my hands and turned my palms upward as we climbed higher and higher. I felt Ben's hand on my arm, and I opened my eyes as we leveled out. Wiping my tears, I sat up and looked left out the window. The horizon sparkled, and I smiled.

"Okay," I breathed and looked up at Ben. "I did it."

"You did it," he squeezed my arm and smiled.

I looked over at the kids. Evan had his head leaned back, his eyes closed. Shelby was nestled into her neck pillow, nearly asleep too. Lily was mouthing the words to whatever was playing in her ears, now oblivious to the world around her.

I took a few pictures with my phone, grateful for all of it: the fear, the tears, the people, the plane. I pulled down my tray and lay my head down on my arms, slipping in and out of the dreamscape until we landed in Florida.

Two nights later, as we sat down to dinner after the wedding ceremony, David got up to speak.

"Good evening, everyone," he called out. "Hi, hi there! Can I have your attention?" The noise under the tent dwindled as my brother began, and my parents took their seats at a nearby table. "Chris and I want to just say thank you for being here. She and I are so grateful for our family and close friends who have made the trip to be with us this week. I know that for some of you, this was particularly challenging, and I want you to know how much I appreciate you being here."

My mom turned to me and whispered, "That's you."

Tears of gratitude welled up in my eyes. I felt seen and appreciated, and I was proud of myself for working through the fear so that I didn't miss out on all the moments the wedding weekend entailed. My kids were having a blast driving around the resort in golf carts, walking the beach barefoot at sunset, the ocean waves kissing their toes. They loved the tennis courts and games, the food and the fun, and of course the time together with uncles and cousins we didn't always get to see.

I returned home grateful and proud, and four months later, I got on a flight to Detroit, this time just me and my kids, to see our extended family for the spring holiday. It was the last flight we took before the world shut down.

Brave Reflection

How we approach each decision that tests our fears and resistance matters. The invitation to surrender will return again and again in our lives in myriad ways. I often find myself having to consider the benefits and the risks, ultimately landing on what I am willing to surrender (e.g., control to the pilots, the chefs, or my circumstances) and paying much closer attention to the benefits I will reap by bravely facing a fear to gain more authority over my choices.

Take a few moments to reflect on what fear has held you back from. Use the following journal prompts to get clarity on what gets in the way and the next step you can take to move forward:

- What dream, project, or experience has fear held you back from?
- What are the benefits of taking a step toward that which you desire?
- How can you practice surrendering to bravely show up for your purpose and for the people in your life?

If you'd like to claim your intention and action step(s) on social media when you're done, use #EveryDayImBrave for more accountability and support. Remember that you can head over to www.everydayimbrave.com to find additional resources to help you along this journey.

11

ALL WAS WELL ENOUGH

I WAS SICK THE WEEK BEFORE spring break in March 2020, just days before the nation shut down because of the COVID-19 pandemic. I didn't have much of a fever, but I was feeling pretty awful and was constantly stifling a horrid hacking cough that kept me from actively teaching much that week while still being present in the classroom. No substitutes were available, and I'd already used up most of my leave that year. At that moment, I wasn't deeply afraid of this new virus. It hadn't reached Iowa yet that we knew of, and I naively hoped that maybe it never would. As the students in our school started teasing one another that every sneeze or sniffle was that weird new flu out there killing people on a cruise ship, I continued to assure them that we were fine.

And we *were* fine . . . until we weren't.

I had left my classroom relatively tidied up before the break and had stacked piles of reading journals into a heap on my desk, believing I'd return to them in a week to finish grading. Instead, they sat there until midsummer, when I came to toss them instead of read them. The building I taught in was undergoing construction, and we had to pack up everything in our rooms. I was temporarily being moved to a different classroom the following year while they redid the floors and cabinets in mine. Teachers were only allowed in the building in preparation for construction, so I came in on my assigned day (masked, sanitized, and temperature-checked) and took home what I knew I didn't want to lose, only to return a month later to move everything into a storage unit and set up shop to teach remotely at home.

What the school year ahead would look like wasn't clear. By then, my children and I had been isolating at home for months—seeing no one outside our immediate family except for a few driveway visits, outdoors and masked with plenty of fresh air and space between us to keep us safe from whatever particles might lurk in the air.

The other complex piece of this unprecedented puzzle was that I had to acknowledge the absolute relief I felt when everything around us closed. Activities were canceled, restaurants became takeout only, and all my groceries were delivered to my front door. I was almost embarrassed to admit it, but when everything halted, it became crystal clear to me that the world I had been out in every day had been frying my nervous system and was clearly taking its toll.

We were constantly on the go. My gaggle of kids and bonus kids were active in the arts, so there was always a show or recital or concert to attend. And if not that, then there was the driving to rehearsal, the late-night dinners, the meetings, the homework, the grading, the dating . . . all of it. When it was clear that we weren't going back to school anytime soon and spring break was extended indefinitely, my family and I (and so many others not deemed "essential workers") were able to take a collective breath. And boy, did we fucking need it.

A lot of my work as a teacher was managing not only my own nervous system but helping to coregulate a room full of teenagers. It was actually a strength of mine, I believe, but it weighed heavily on me. If that was my only job—if I could have worked on social–emotional well-being and success strategies all day long with my students—I might have been less burned out. But being a teacher entails so much more than that. There were lesson plans, professional development, district goals, assessments, the political landscape, homework, chaperoning, breaking up fights, soothing tears, talking through drama, teaching and reteaching . . . and then suddenly this strange new virus was making its way around the world? It was a lot.

So as our state government battled with new legislation about mask-wearing, block schedules, and remote learning, I knew I couldn't leave anything to chance. Fear demanded that I stay home, and I could make that happen in only one of two ways: quit my job or document my diagnosis for disability accommodations.

I was going to have to document my fear, remove the (metaphorical) mask, and officially announce through an Americans with Disabilities Act (ADA) reasonable accommodation request form that I wasn't mentally well enough to return to the school building. That was difficult, but I didn't see any other way to work from home without quitting my job entirely and finding something else remote.

Dr. Temple and I set up a telehealth appointment to chat before school started. He was hesitant to complete a disability form for me even though that ADA form was required for the district to even consider me for a fully online position. Dr. Temple wanted to be sure that the way he wrote that letter outlined *the possibility* of an uptick in my symptoms rather than a declaration that my having OCD would make it difficult to work. He was a brilliant, kind man who knew (even when I didn't) that setting up an ADA request could have long-lasting underlying ramifications for my psyche, potentially creating more fuel for the subconscious beliefs that would hold me prisoner to fear. He didn't want to box me in by declaring that OCD and anxiety impaired my ability to do my job well, especially because that wouldn't always be true. He wanted me to rest in the evidence of the work we'd previously done and the trust we had in my ability to overcome and manage OCD symptoms as they came.

But I had drawn a very thick line in the sand. I could not and *would not* go into a building with hundreds of people. My brain said, *No, no, no. No way. I just can't.* And so I didn't. With Dr. Temple's letter, I was one of the very few in our district who were granted a fully online position that year, even though I certainly was not the only one afraid to return in person.

The letter was also pretty accurate the way he wrote it. The pandemic *did* create an uptick in my OCD and anxiety symptoms. It was scary for most of us, so it seems only logical that it would be for me too. One Sunday evening, just before our socially distanced family dinner, my mom was recounting her experience at the doctor's office earlier that week, noting how hypervigilant she'd been sitting in the waiting room.

"When I first got there," she described, "I looked around to make sure everyone else in the room was masked and seated more than six feet apart." She went on to say that she had noticed a man who had most of his mask just dangling off his chin, so she had chosen the seat farthest from him. "I was about to pick up a magazine on the display table next to me," she added, "but then I stopped. I didn't know who had touched them, thinking about all the hands that flipped through the pages."

"And then," she went on, "the woman behind the front desk started coughing! I was so uncomfortable, so I just pulled out a mini-bottle of hand sanitizer from my purse and slathered it on. I was just *so* preoccupied watching what everyone was doing, what they were touching, how close they were to me."

I chuckled. "Yeah, kind of consuming, isn't it?" I looked up from my plate.

"Yeah, it was. I mean, I never used to even care and now—" she stopped.

"Welcome to my world," I sighed.

I certainly wouldn't wish OCD on anyone, but it was interesting to listen to the experiences of others, like my mom, and have these stories mirror back to me the thoughts, fears, and rituals that I'd been holding on to for nearly two decades prior to the pandemic. So many people were hypervigilant and afraid to leave their homes. But as the months passed, that changed: There were new vaccines and new antivirals, and people just stopped letting the fear of getting sick run their lives. Folks began to gather, schools reopened, activities began functioning as they had before, and fewer and fewer people masked, tested, and isolated.

So although that rise in my OCD symptoms wasn't a surprise, neither Dr. Temple nor I could predict the profound effect the pandemic would have on my ability to return to life outside my home once the worst was over and the world reopened.

Midway through the early months of the pandemic, Ben and I bought a house together. With so much uncertainty out in the world, we were even more committed to the support and love that our relationship provided one another. When COVID-19 reached our inner circle, my world became even smaller than before. Ben's daughter, who spent half her time at school in the hybrid model, came down with it while at her mom's house. Then, shortly after, Nick and his wife, who were spending regular time with the kids, got it. I feared every outing, even masked, that my extended family partook in. I was afraid not only of getting sick but also that one of us might pass it on to my parents; both of them had survived cancer and were well over seventy, and though not immunocompromised, they were certainly at higher risk for complications.

I started relying more heavily on my tools to not freak out every moment of every day. It wasn't enough. I called Dr. Temple and started to see him regularly again via telehealth. I couldn't shut myself off from the world entirely, though that's exactly what I was doing. Moreover, I knew I couldn't ask those around me to stay home and isolate when it was no longer deemed necessary by the government or health-care professionals.

Here I was—thirteen years since the onset of severe OCD, ten years since my official diagnosis, and eight years since beginning CBT and racking up wins—now living in a postpandemic era. At its worst, a lot of people were carrying hand sanitizer, wiping off their groceries, and forgoing handshakes without question. But as others moved on from the moment, I became solidly stuck in these rituals.

From the view outside my new home office window, everything was serene. I didn't have to worry about what I touched or the air I was breathing because I knew it was safe. I could use my own bathroom. I could eat my own food, untouched and un-breathed on by anyone else except, perhaps, the people in my house, who were well trained and knew better. This sense of safety was an illusion, of course; the reality was that our house just had a much greater probability of being safe. There was no guarantee that the air in my home didn't carry virus particles, but it was certainly *safer* than the doctor's office or the local drugstore where people bought their cough medicine.

Prior to the pandemic, I was rarely home. I worked in a building with eight hundred people. I traveled with my son to show choir and dance competitions. I hung out at bars and restaurants with friends and played music. I went to the movies. I attended workshops. I frequented places with people breathing and singing and laughing and hugging. But now, a big part of me just wanted to stay home forever. It didn't matter how lonely or depressed I got. It didn't matter how bored I was. It didn't matter how frustrated my family was. I just couldn't see how it would be worth the risk. I wanted to avoid going out into the world at all costs. I even fantasized about building a "she shed" in my backyard, a little house that only I'd be able to enter, with full plumbing installed and a place for snacks. I wouldn't have to spray Lysol or wipe down all the cabinet, drawer, and door handles multiple times a day because it would just be me—my own germs, my own air. I'd be free from danger in that little house all by myself.

But that, of course, while fun to think about on the surface, was actually really lonely and sad underneath it all. It would mean that OCD had won and I'd be alone.

When Dr. Temple and I were in session, he helped me look at this dilemma more closely. He posited that the question I was continually asking had to shift from *How safe or how clean is this?* to *How much weight should the desire for safety be given in this scenario?*

Ultimately, I had to ask myself, *Should safety and cleanliness be the driving force behind my decisions?* My wise mind, an idea introduced to me by Dr. Temple, would of course say it needed to matter far less, but the fearful, worried parts of me fought hard, dug their heels in, and shouted about all the ways in which catastrophe could happen if I extended my physical reach back into the community around me.

Together, Dr. Temple and I continued to reframe my thoughts for each new challenge in front of me: the kids returning to after-school activities, my son contracting COVID from a choir concert, an invitation to sing again with my band that I ultimately turned down. Each scenario entailed conflict, turmoil, bravery, and grace.

We worked on trust and reframing—and then, we had the difficult task of saying goodbye. Our decade of working together came to a close with his retirement in December 2020. With his support in those final months together, I felt more confident and ready to take some baby steps forward. I had more tools with which to accompany Evan to his dance competitions that spring, to show up masked and courageous for Shelby's theatre productions, and to lead by example and encourage Lily to attend school half-time the following year, understanding the importance of social contact along with the online schooling she'd been receiving. The new year ahead would start with an abundance of gratitude for Dr. Temple and all the tools, support, and kindness he'd brought to me. He changed my life for the better, and I'm so grateful for that. For a moment in time, all was well enough.

Brave Reflection

Whether we're enduring a pandemic, a community tragedy, or a really difficult transition at home, we must recognize how trauma and stressful circumstances affect our well-being and ultimately challenge us to learn and grow from them once we come out of survival mode. We have to recognize and acknowledge the pain, frustration, and fear that come with challenges like these, and we also have to take steps to move through and learn from what the experience is teaching us.

Take some time to reflect on how you can process a challenging situation by using the following journal prompts:

- What have you understood differently now that time has passed and you can see this situation from a higher perspective?
- How can you reemerge after catastrophe, trauma, or collective pain? What do you need to feel supported and ready to do something differently?
- How can you shift from fear to feeling safe enough or well enough so that you can stairstep the healing process and move through the world one moment at a time?

Share your shifts on social media with #EveryDayImBrave to celebrate your resiliency and wisdom. Then, you can head over to www.everydayimbrave.com to check out additional resources.

12

UNZIP MY SKIN

AS I CONTINUED TO SLOWLY ADAPT to life outside the confines of my bubble, things inside me spiraled downward. I could barely leave my house, except for absolutely necessary events for my kids. Even *at* home, the anxiety and panic overwhelmed me at times, leaving me feeling pretty worthless, irritable, and probably not that much fun to be around most days. I could no longer reasonably request that my family stay home, stay masked, and not live their lives. Every sniffle, sneeze, or cough still sounded an alarm in my head. Moreover, because I couldn't control the outside world, I dipped back into habits that feigned control over my inner world.

How could I keep the germs at bay? Don't touch; wash. Don't ingest; wash. Don't go; wash.

And out in the world? Mask, keep my distance, sanitize, wash, wash, wash.

Simultaneously, I tumbled back down the rabbit hole of food avoidance because of fear of contamination and was skirting around dangerous territory with my eating. The weight started coming off, and the headaches rebounded. This time around, though, I knew I had to maintain enough calories most of the time, and I tried to find substitutions for foods quickly being taken off my safe-to-eat list. I knew I needed to have enough sustenance even if there was very little variety.

The challenges didn't stop there.

It started as just a quick flash in my mind: I'd envision the skin atop my head splitting down the middle and slowly slipping off my skull, just like you'd see in a cartoon. It was like a human suit of sorts: the top layer of myself, sliding down either side of my face and flopping onto my shoulders. It wasn't really scary. I didn't see a skeleton of myself in my mind but rather another face that was still my own.

The repetition of this image came more frequently and during quiet moments of the day, when I was doing the dishes or folding laundry. Sometimes the skin would unzip all the way down the middle of my chest, ribs exposed and heart beating. My skin lay around my hips, appearing like a sweatshirt tied around my waist.

I didn't have any urge or desire to tear off my skin in real life, which is a key piece to OCD intrusive thoughts: While they can be disturbing, they are generally harmless. Thoughts like these can be scary, which is why they are defined as intrusive. They interrupt your awareness; they intrude on your peace, appearing suddenly and repeatedly in your consciousness. When my symptoms were at their worst, I could have a few moments of panic from an intrusive thought—for instance, at the kitchen sink, where I'd wash the knives and "see" myself filet my own flesh—but I trusted myself not to go there because I recognized these thoughts for what they were. Understanding the components of OCD symptoms helped me gain that perspective, and Dr. Temple helped me recognize that they were just thoughts and that they would pass faster and be less disruptive if I just let them float by.

When the image of unzipping my skin repeated a few more times, I wondered if it was metaphorical. The message was potent and clear: It was time to shed this layer. It was time to focus on becoming the next version of myself, to become the one who doesn't allow fear to call the shots anymore, to become the one who deepens her connections, steps out of her comfort zone, and shows up in leadership in a fundamentally new way. It was time to shed the skin of fear and truly create a life I loved.

I began with curiosity: How many layers of this fear that I wear are my own? Where do these thick rows of panic in my brain begin? What is the purpose of this suffering? How can I lessen its hold?

I think about my mom: She is not a fan of interstate driving or flying much either, but she continues to travel and live life bravely. As a kid, I'd often observe her tears on takeoff, or I'd watch her flinch as we passed a semitruck, grasping tightly to the armrest pulling her out of an imagined harm's way. I'm sure it affected me at the time, sending a message that these were things to fear and feeling sad at my mom's suffering, but today, I realize that what it truly taught me was resilience and courage. I'm grateful for learning both from her.

My mom would also frequently mention Papa, her father, and how he had a terrible fear of heights. "It's genetic, I think," she would say, and when the Human Genome Project began to uncover all sorts of coding in our DNA that made us more susceptible to turning different traits on and off, such as agoraphobia and general anxiety,[1] her theory became fact.

When I began having panic attacks in the shower years ago, feeling the world beneath my feet giving way to nothingness, I knew the fear was even deeper than that. As more research in genetics gave way to the study of epigenetics, it revealed that environmental factors, traumas, and other stressors can actually change how genes are expressed.[2] When I learned this, I wondered how much of the fear I carried was the result of ancestral trauma. If those changes in how a gene is expressed can also then be inherited by future generations, then it made sense to me that I'd be more prone to anxiety and the desire to seek feelings of safety because it was buried in my genetic coding. There were many in my family tree

---

1 Nora I. Strom, Brad Verhulst, Silviu-Alin Bacanu, et al., "Genome-Wide Association Study of Major Anxiety Disorders in 122,341 European-Ancestry Cases Identifies 58 Loci and Highlights GABAergic Signaling," preprint, medRxiv, July 5, 2024, https://doi.org/10.1101/2024.07.03.24309466.

2 Raymond R. Crowe, "The Genetics of the Phobic Disorders and Generalized Anxiety Disorder," in *Principles of Psychiatric Genetics*, ed. John I. Nurnbuerger Jr. and Wade Berrettini (Cambridge University Press, 2012).

who had perished in Holocaust mass graves, gas showers, and concen-
tration camps, yet those who had survived and experienced the fear and
trauma not only told stories so that we'd never forget but also potentially
changed our genetic expression related to fear. I knew within my lineage
(and so many others') that we carried the collective weight of fear and
loss of autonomy and control.

These fears were deeper than the outer experiences of heights, germs,
and airplanes. The further inward I looked, the more I understood that
what I also struggled with was who I would be without fear. And the
questions followed:

What if this fear wasn't even mine?

*What if the layers I continued to peel off revealed a me I did not know or
understand?*

What if it hurt to unbury the truth of who I am? What was that truth?

What if other people don't like who I become?

What if, what if, what if . . .

I heard Dr. Temple's voice echo in my mind, "Does the benefit outweigh the risk?" What was the benefit here? What good could come from
me releasing even more layers of fear? What if I wanted to become someone
who did things she desired to do regardless of fear? How could I begin to
not only understand but also believe that the comfort and familiarity of fear
weren't serving me any longer? Fear may have been all I'd ever known, but it
didn't have to be the only thing I was. And so these questions shifted from
the risks to the benefits:

*What if becoming the truth of who I am allows me to connect deeper with
every soul I meet?*

What if becoming the truth of who I am allows others to do the same?

*What if, without fear dictating all my actions, I am able to live with more
joy, more love, more laughter, and more creativity?*

This shift in perspective from the negative *what ifs* to the positive helped
me get unstuck. The only other questions left were these: How do I get
there? How do I begin to believe that the version of who I dream to become

has worth or value? How do I get the support I need to move through the debilitating present moment and step bravely into my future self?

The answer, of course, came back to willingness: I had to be willing to take the risk, do the work, use the tools, and get the support I needed so that I could step more fully into the next best version of myself.

At our last appointment before his retirement, Dr. Temple made sure I'd have a phone number for another CBT therapist in my back pocket in case I'd need it. He referred me to a practitioner he had previously mentored and knew we would be a good fit. One afternoon, sitting in the Walgreens parking lot after a particularly challenging half hour trying to decide on a safe snack to buy, I called the number and got the office voicemail.

"Hi. My name is Renee Zukin," I paused, not quite knowing what to say. "I got Zach Pacha's number from Dr. Temple, who said I should connect with him. I don't know if he is accepting new patients, but I'd like to meet him and see about possible next steps. Thanks. Bye."

I hung up and burst into tears. The first step is often the hardest, but once taken, it can set you on a whole new path.

It took six more months to get my first appointment. It turns out that the health-care system has some cracks, especially when it comes to getting good mental health support. But this isn't a new problem, and that conversation is for another time.

Zach was no slouch. His office was about two hours away, so we met via telehealth—which was okay by me for all sorts of obvious reasons. I was still only leaving my house when absolutely necessary to drive a kid to activities or to hit the coffee shop drive-through. We were close in age and demeanor. We had a similar sense of humor and shared a lot of the same '80s references in our conversations, and his straightforward and quirky approach helped me feel connected, understood, and able to dive quickly into the work at hand.

Zach also had an in-depth and structured approach to diagnosis and treatment that brought to light some real truths I wasn't facing about how closed-in my life had really become. Seeing bits of myself quantified in new ways through these comprehensive intake forms was eye-opening. I filled out little bubble sheets identifying how often I'd have catastrophic thoughts and what kinds, marking off list after list of obsessive concerns and how incapacitated (or not) they made me feel. One survey I took had me rank how anxious everyday activities made me feel, such as running up a flight of stairs, being in a stuffy conference room, taking a shower, or shopping at the mall. On a scale of zero to ten, most of the things on that list ranked seven or higher.

I also had to rank places and spaces that were likely to make me feel panic sensations. Different from just general anxiety or nerves, panic sensations were very physical: dissociation, vertigo, tachycardia, weakness in the limbs. I'd often feel disoriented, suffer from tunnel vision, and feel much like Alice did while in Wonderland. I put checkmarks next to examples such as waiting in lines, large crowds, big box stores, and wide-open spaces. And then I had to write down how literally far I felt willing and able to go from my home, which turned out to be quite a small radius of just a few miles without some serious anxiety developing.

It's one thing to feel the anxiety of these places and experiences; it's another to see them all add up to additional official diagnoses of agoraphobia and panic disorder.

Agoraphobia is the "intense fear and anxiety of any place or situation where escape might be difficult. Agoraphobia involves avoidance of situations such as being alone outside of the home; traveling in a car, bus, or airplane; or being in a crowded area";[3] in my case, it came on more fully because of OCD. Panic disorder didn't surprise me as much; it is defined as "frequent and unexpected panic attacks. [Panic] attacks are characterized by a sudden wave of fear or discomfort or a sense of losing control even when there is no clear danger or trigger."[4] What had shifted for me,

3   "Agoraphobia," National Institute of Mental Health, accessed January 4, 2025, https://www.nimh
     .nih.gov/health/statistics/agoraphobia.

4   "Panic Disorder: When Fear Overwhelms," National Institute of Mental Health, accessed
     January 4, 2025, https://www.nimh.nih.gov/health/publications/panic-disorder-when-fear
     -overwhelms#part_6101.

however, was the intensity beyond just feeling anxious and uncomfortable and how often I was experiencing these episodes that I desperately wanted to avoid.

Central to the experience of OCD, anxiety, panic, and phobias is often doing whatever it takes to avoid the things that trigger panic attacks in the first place. The problem for me was that the list of things that often triggered panic attacks grew so expansive, I realized that instead of creating a beautiful safe bubble to exist in, I had just spent the last two years rebuilding the bars of a prison I'd already escaped from once before.

Looking at the intake surveys Zach had provided left me no choice but to see just how far down the rabbit hole I'd gone in a number of areas of my life. I'd been working remotely, and everything I needed was pretty close at hand, so I didn't think my life was suffering that much from OCD and anxiety.

The numbers revealed a different story. My son, now seventeen, was the one driving us to his dance competitions because I no longer could navigate the interstate without feeling like the Earth was turning and I couldn't see. I'd have headaches for days because I was too afraid to eat more than a few foods from my safe list, which also wreaked havoc on my gut. I had to be willing to accept the reality of where I was and then take the next step forward.

Zach utilized a combination of CBT and exposure work, much like Dr. Temple did, but it looked pretty different for panic disorder. Similarly, I came to our sessions with a lot of resistance, just as I had done with Dr. Temple, but I learned to recognize it for what it was and return to the question of willingness.

Our work began with some of the weirdest activities I'd ever heard of, but the goal was to expose myself first to panic symptoms themselves and not the things that trigger panic to begin with. I didn't really understand it at first, but I played along.

"Are you willing to breathe through a straw for thirty seconds?" he asked.

"A straw?" I laughed. "Sure."

"Well," he said. "I guess first, do you have any coffee straws in your house?"

"Um, I might?" I answered. I took my laptop to the kitchen with me and set it on the counter while I searched the drawers.

"Found some regular straws; will that work?" I called over to the screen.

"For now," he said. "Go ahead and cut one in half so it's smaller."

I unwrapped the straw, cognizant of where my fingers were touching it, and paused. "Am I going to be putting this in my mouth?" I asked. I watched as he confirmed with a nod. "Okay," I said, "I have to wash my hands, then."

"No, you don't," he declared. I got closer to the screen and glared at his telehealth square.

"Yes, I do," I insisted. "I can't put the end I'm about to cut with the scissors in my mouth, and I have to hold the other end while I cut it, so . . ."

I waited for my excuses to land with some sort of agreement.

"That's a choice you're making. You can hang on to that safety behavior for today," Zach said. He wasn't interested in tiptoeing around the obvious.

I looked at the half-unwrapped straw in my left hand, noting that my fingers were still only touching the paper wrapping. I grabbed the scissors off the counter with my right hand and cut the straw straight down the middle. The half still in the wrapper was safe. I'd use that end for the exercise and skip the handwashing.

"Ha!" I snickered back at him as I held the straw up for him to see. He rolled his eyes.

Back in my office chair, he reviewed the instructions for the exercise. He was going to set a timer, and I was to breathe through the straw until the timer went off. It seemed easy enough.

"Ready?" he asked. I nodded, the clean end of the straw now in my mouth. "Go," he commanded.

A few seconds in, I felt my chest tighten and my heart begin to race. I immediately understood the assignment. *Oh, this is why we are doing this . . . Okay, Renee, focus on the air going in and out of your mouth.* I continued to talk myself through it in my mind. *Count to four. 1 . . . 2 . . . That's it; slow it down . . . 3 . . . 4 . . . You're getting air. You are getting the oxygen you need.*

My heart slowed; my mind quieted. The timer beeped. "Done," he said. "How was that?"

I explained what I had felt, what I had gone through, and how I had reframed the moment.

"Good," he affirmed. "You've got some tools, and you're using them. And you're right: This exercise is meant to mimic the sensation of not being able to breathe, something that happens a lot with claustrophobia or other panic sensations. Are you willing to try a minute?"

I consented. The second time was easier now that I knew what to expect, knowing that I was the one deciding to move further in this work—knowing that my willingness, my consent, was vital to healing because it had been taken from me all those years ago on the apartment floor and, again and again, every time I allowed someone else's desires to matter more than my discomfort.

"Great," he said. "Let's do it again, only this time, I want you to walk around the room while you're doing it."

"Just, like, back and forth in the room?" I confirmed.

"Yep. You ready?" he asked. I nodded. "Go," he said.

I stood up, straw in mouth, and walked back and forth in front of my desk. I continued the reframed thoughts in my mind: *I'm getting all the oxygen I need. I can breathe through this straw.*

In the following weeks, we worked a few more rounds, adding different conditions as I went: a thick winter coat, a scarf wrapped around my face—mimicking hot, stuffy elements that might make it feel harder to breathe. The more conditions he added, such as one shoe on and one shoe off to feel the ground uneven beneath me, the more important it was for me to notice.

What I noticed was that in a knowingly safe environment, these physical panic sensations were *not* harmful or dangerous. In fact, the more we did the work, the more the physical responses became less and less bothersome. I had to notice that panic sensations were not only survivable but also changeable. I also had to understand that what I feared most was the feeling of fear rather than the possibility of whatever I was afraid of happening—*actually* happening.

In other words, he said, "The fear of what *might* happen, what it *might* feel like, is usually worse than the experience itself."

I locked that new thought into a mantra that I could return to: *Panic sensations are not dangerous.* This helped me not latch on to the thoughts that something horrible was happening inside my body. It helped me allow the feelings to occur, move through me, and dissipate. As we began to tackle each new activity and real-life experiences week by week, this mantra helped me increase my ability to do daily tasks with far more ease. My perception of what I was able and willing to do shifted. Was I unafraid? No, but I was willing, and I was brave.

Layer by layer, like the skin of a molted snake, I shed parts of myself in order to grow. Renewal is part of our evolution. My first name, Renee, actually means *reborn*, and I used to believe that meant I'd have to continually change my outer world in order to create a new life for myself: the new job, the new relationship, the new house. What I now understand is that it takes deep inner work to create lasting, fulfilling outer change.

It's not an easy task, especially when those around you expect you to stay the same. When you begin to make different choices for yourself, even something as simple as giving up your morning cup of coffee, it can be an adjustment for those around you as well. Suddenly, you're no longer the person who drinks coffee anymore, and that makes them wonder, usually subconsciously, *What else about you is going to change?*

It's natural to notice constriction during times of change; resistance comes up to preserve the status quo. To *be* better, though, we have to *do* better. When it comes to OCD and anxiety, there isn't necessarily a cure, but there is better. When we show up willing to look through the lens of curiosity and brave enough to surrender to the fear, we can continue to take action toward creating a better life for ourselves, not just in spite of our diagnoses but often because of them.

Brave Reflection

To be better, we often have to let go of old stories, taking on parts of a new identity that doesn't allow fear to call the shots. Our thoughts are like habits: They may be deeply ingrained, but they *are* changeable. You can feel the difference when you're ready to let go of what is no longer serving you. The thoughts may feel wrong, or you might even start feeling annoyed at having them, hearing yourself say things repeatedly that just don't matter as much as they used to.

Take a few moments to reflect on what you may be ready to let go of. What are some experiences you've always wanted to have but feel are impossible to create? What if you tried having a new thought about them? Use the following questions to journal and see what shifts for you:

- What is something you've always wanted to do, but it felt nearly impossible?
- What would have to change for you to be able to think about the first step in having that experience?
- What do you want to make more room for in your life? Are there parts of you that you're ready to let go of?

What new ideas or perspectives became clear for you as you wrote? Share your new thoughts with #EveryDayImBrave on social media to lock in this new perspective of hope and possibility. Check out further materials and support at www.everydayimbrave.com.

13

PHOENIX RISING

IN NOVEMBER OF 2022, MY SON told me about a trip to Phoenix he wanted to take for a national tap dance festival that was happening just after the new year. One of his former teachers was leading a couple of workshops there alongside other amazing tap dance professionals, and he really wanted to go. I wanted to support my son's goals and dreams. I wanted him to not fear the future. I wanted him to stay brave and curious.

"We will figure out a way to get you there," I told him, unsure of what that was going to look like. Sure, he was newly eighteen and could technically go by himself, though he wasn't yet old enough to rent a car or even check into a hotel.

I also didn't like the idea of him traveling alone or being so far away from home in case he needed something. Yes, I could surrender to the knowledge that there were other adults there leading the festival and dance moms who would help him out if needed, but the reality was that I really *wanted* to be with him on this adventure. It was new to feel that kind of desire not just stemming from fear of him being alone or hurt or sick. I was proud that my initial response to the idea wasn't just a loud internal *no way*. This was postpandemic progress.

We talked through different options to get there. I'd not been on an airplane since the pandemic. The thought of being in close quarters with a bunch of strangers on a plane seemed nearly impossible, not to mention that I had been dealing with severe panic attacks when I ventured out even close to home. Evan and I looked at trains, but there were almost no direct routes between Iowa and Arizona, and it would take days to make the 1,500-mile trek. I thought about people who could fly with him instead of me, friends or other dancers who might be going, but no one was headed that way. I mapped out the drive, through mountains and deserts, which would have been a long haul for us in the middle of winter. There was no easy answer, and I felt like there was no other choice but to get back on an airplane and join my son (and bring along his siblings) on this adventure. It was important for me to align with the kind of mother I wanted to be. I had to show up. I had to be *willing* to go.

Much like a diamond created by pressure, the way toward deeper transformation opened up further. I had to shed another layer of fear because my relationships mattered to me. Similar to how I felt it was important to show up for my brother's wedding, I knew I needed to show up for my son. By looking at and understanding the values that I wanted to live by—the importance of showing up and supporting my family and my friends—I saw how much fear had truly gotten in the way of me forming and sustaining so many relationships throughout my adult life. If I wanted to call myself a good mom and a good friend while living the integrity of that value, then I had to continue to be there for them, even when it felt scary to do so.

Zach and I spent the next few sessions on things related to the fears I had in general and the ones that would follow me to Arizona: fear of falling, fear of eating, fear of getting sick or others being sick, fear of the airplane ride, and, of course, the fear of fear itself.

I had to make a conscious choice with each step of the journey. It began with simply choosing to say yes, then being willing to book the tickets, the hotel, and the car. As each day passed, I got waves of anxiety whenever I thought about getting back on an airplane or worried about what I'd be able to eat, but then, I would take time to reframe the thoughts, refocus on what was right in front of me in the moment, and trust that I'd figure it out along the way.

This trip itself was really was a no-brainer when it came to tangible benefits: warmer weather in the middle of winter; seeing my son be challenged and thrive doing what he loves; taking my youngest to the doorstep of her best friend, who had moved to Phoenix a few years prior; and spending dedicated time with my eldest daughter as we explored new places. These benefits and more far outweighed the real *and* perceived risks.

When we arrived at the airport, I was okay. I was anxious, of course, but willing and just staying present as we moved through security and waited at the gate. Once boarded, the kids and I took up most of the row—Shelby in the aisle seat on the right, while I nestled in with my mask on between Evan and Lily on the left. I looked out the window at the snow glistening across the farmland and said a prayer of gratitude for the warmth we were about to experience in Arizona.

Staying focused on the rewards and benefits ahead, I turned to each of my kids, air-kissed my hand, and placed it on their foreheads one at a time. "I love you . . . I love you . . . and I love you," I said. It was a ritual I'd started when they were little before any long car ride that we took along the interstate. I believed that the extra love and the imaginary bubble of light I'd surround them with as I touched their heads would keep us all safe. I still do, and as young adults now, they humor me. Not all rituals are related to OCD, and not all OCD rituals are inherently negative. What matters more when it comes to OCD is how one feels if the ritual isn't completed. At different points in my life, not completing this "I love you" ritual would bring up enormous amounts of anxiety. I once stopped the car on the side of the road just to make my rounds around the car before we went any farther because I didn't feel safe enough without having done it. Now, I do it because it allows me a moment of connection with my family, and if I forget, it's not a big deal.

We arrived in Phoenix and made our way to the rental car office. Evan and Shelby argued over who would be the second driver until I reminded them that Evan wasn't even old enough to legally operate the rental. I would drive us to Scottsdale, we'd settle into our hotel room, and we would be okay.

What I've noticed now is that it's almost easier to navigate some of the fears when I'm traveling. I have no choice but to eat foods from restaurants or kitchens that aren't my own. I have to summon the bravery to navigate the interstate and get us to our destinations. I have to hold myself to a higher standard, which both frightens and encourages me to show up with more courage than at home because there isn't the safety net to fall back into.

The next morning, we ate breakfast at the hotel, dropped Evan off at the dance studio, and waited in the parking lot for Lily's friend and her dad to arrive. Lily and her best friend hadn't seen one another in person since the move, and it was a reunion to behold. Both kids were a little awkward as we all took turns hugging one another and taking pictures, noting how big they'd gotten. There was a full day of fun planned, and Lily's friend and her father whisked Lily off for the adventure ahead.

Shelby and I looked at one another. "Well," I said, "what should we do today?"

It was a rare gift for us to have this one-on-one time together and really be present without other responsibilities or work to muddle through.

"I was looking at some different touristy places online, and I found this," she held her phone out for me to take a look. "It could be fun?"

I tilted the phone out of direct sunlight and focused on the photo of a giant cactus along a dirt path. "Desert Botanical Garden," I read aloud. Shelby had become something of a master gardener via online classes during the pandemic, and I loved supporting her new interest. "That could be *so* fun!"

Cacti had a special meaning for me. When Ben and I had first started dating years prior, he had noted that my hands were very, very dry (an ongoing problem with compulsive handwashing). He started calling me Cactus Hands in a loving way, and I'd refer to him as Bear, his big frame and even bigger heart being a comfort early on. When we texted, we used the bear and cactus emojis to refer to one another, and then we started seeing bears and cacti next to one another everywhere: T-shirts in a storefront window, journals on display at the department store, advertisements on TV and in movies. Even a new friend of ours shocked us when showing off his tattoos: a bear on one arm, a cactus on the other. We took these synchronicities to be affirmations of what we already knew to be true, and years later, we are still getting gifts from our kids with bear- and cactus--themed images.

The cactus metaphor went deeper too. As you know, it's pretty hard to get too close to a cactus; their spines work well to keep people at arm's length. It was just as difficult for me to get close to people in a deeply intimate way, both physically and emotionally. The shame and perceived burden of having OCD would get in the way, not to mention the fear of contamination that it held over me.

One summer, Ben's daughter picked out a book for me as a gift called *Nobody Hugs a Cactus*, by Carter Goodrich.[1] She was only seven years old then and so thoughtful, having asked Ben immediately when they saw it to get it for me while they were on a shopping trip to buy her big brother new shoes. I hugged her when she gave it to me, and we read it together that evening. As I did so, I struggled to hold back the tears.

Hank, the main character in the book, was a cactus. He liked things clean and quiet, and he didn't want to be disturbed. It turned out, though, that cranky little Hank was actually feeling kinda lonely, and as each desert animal traveled on by, it became clear that he wasn't as happy with being alone as he once thought.

I recognized myself in Hank. There were parts of me that feared germs, feared closeness, and liked everything in its place. There were also parts of me that understood that I had been feeling pretty lonely and isolated,

---

1 Carter Goodrich, *Nobody Hugs a Cactus* (Simon & Schuster Books for Young Readers, 2019).

denying myself both food and love in a lot of ways. This incessant quest to control everything ended with an empty treasure chest. Without the messiness of life, I was missing out on deeper connections and more joy.

Shelby and I arrived at the Desert Botanical Garden and started down the trail. The pathways were filled with cacti large and small. Some flowered beautifully; others wrapped raggedly around the earth, their pokey tendrils reaching toward an unseen force. What struck me as we walked through the gardens and learned about the different species of cactus was just how resilient they are. They survive in the harshest environments, different from other plants and animals across the globe. Cacti can last months without water, survive massive heat waves, and still find ways to grow and thrive. Many of them even held actual scars on their limbs, the elements leaving their mark and the cacti showing them off with pride.

Living with a mental health diagnosis feels much the same. Sometimes, the conditions are harsh, and there are moments when we want to hide or give up and give in, but we have to remember the strength that is created when we are able to see the beauty in the way we are made. We also have to find the courage to accept and love where we are at any given moment so that we can find a new path for our tendrils to travel down. From there, we can sprout new flowers, and as the Earth continues to revolve around the sun, we must understand that even though life can be scary, we can continue to show up bravely every day.

As we neared the end of our self-guided tour, I ran like a child to the giant saguaro cactus that marked the entry and exit point. It stood as a giant oak tree might, with its strength and power stunning against the bright blue desert sky. I stood at its base and looked upward, my gaze following its thick trunk nearly fifty feet in the air, and felt a deep kinship. "It's me!" I gleefully called out to Shelby. She snapped a couple pictures while I posed, arms reaching upward toward the cactus's top.

As the sun set that evening, we headed back to the dance studio to watch Evan perform what he'd been learning all day. We then drove south to get Lily and headed back to the hotel. We all slept hard and got up to do it all again the next day.

Even before the trip was over, I felt renewed, transformed. It wasn't lost on me as we packed up to head back to Iowa that Phoenix was not only a geographical place but also a metaphor for the evolution that had just taken place simply from choosing to take this trip. The phoenix rising is a mythical bird that symbolizes renewal and rebirth. From a fire that burns all that is no longer needed, the majestic bird rises with new wings, its strength and beauty unfolding.

Throughout the trip, there were definitely moments of anxiety and fear, but I managed them with the tools I'd been learning the last decade, and I wasn't doing it alone. My kids are my greatest motivation for being a better version of myself, to continually try to offer them an example of what it looks like to meet challenges as they come, to get support when needed, and to keep showing up for one another and meet oneself with compassion, even when it's hard. Like the phoenix rising from the ashes, we can begin again, anew.

Brave Reflection

We are constantly evolving; each new challenge or experience in our lives gives us an opportunity to rise anew from the proverbial ashes. For me, I had to be willing to show up for the people in my life and lean into the belief that I could do so imperfectly. We can become a different, better version of ourselves. We can create new moments, experiences, and connections that allow us to step into our lives more fully, bravely revealing our scars, willing to allow others in.

In this next reflection, think about a time you have come through a challenge feeling stronger and more confident. Or consider what it might feel like to do so with a current challenge. Then, use the following fill-in-the-blank journal prompts:

- A challenge I have been through that has allowed me to show up stronger and wiser than before is _____ _____.

- When I get to the other side of this current challenging situation, I want to feel _____.

- Even though I feel _____, I can show up authentically and connect with the people in my life because _____.

Use #EveryDayImBrave to share your thoughts on social media and be celebrated for how far you've come and where you are aiming to go. Embracing your authenticity and imperfection allows you to express yourself more fully. Check out www.everydayimbrave.com for different ways you can bravely express yourself.

14

NORTHERN LIGHTS

I RETURNED HOME FROM PHOENIX WITH a newfound sense of freedom, joy, and connection, recognizing that these were experiences I'd been deeply longing for without even realizing it. Not long after returning home, I was greeted with the next opportunity to work these new travel muscles, and I had an even braver choice to make.

The business mentoring program I'd been a part of for about three years (and would later begin coaching for) was offering their spring retreat in California as a hybrid event. My colleagues and friends from all over the world, women I'd been working with remotely, would have a chance to gather for the first time since the COVID pandemic halted in-person events everywhere in the country.

I cried when the announcement was made during our group training call on Zoom. Here I was, able to fly with my family, effectively taking the risk alongside them and with their full support, and now, the next layer of this particular onion was already being peeled away.

Would I be able to get on an airplane by myself? Would I be able to travel thousands of miles away from my kids without a massive freak-out? Would I get lost? Get hurt? Die? How would I eat for five days? Where would I stay? Would I have to share a room with other people? Could I even do that if I had to? What if I got sick? What if, what if, what if . . .

The internal alarms were going off loud. I noticed the Zoom chat scrolling by, each message an exclamation of joy, my colleagues eager to buy their plane tickets and make their hotel reservations. I heard the delicate buzz of my phone and looked down. My closest business sisters began texting me, some of them not yet privy to the abundance of anxiety that an opportunity like this presented for me. "Are you gonna go to California?" they asked. "Should we find a place together? We will finally get to hug!!"

"Fuck!" I grumbled.

I turned off my video and crumbled at my desk, wailing cries that released all the complex emotions I was feeling. I'd been so lonely. I was grateful, of course, for the virtual technology that allowed me to gain amazing friends and confidants who had helped me build my business, helped me believe in myself, helped me understand that the vision of my dream life was possible. We cheered each other on as we built those lives for ourselves one small supported step at a time. But life outside my computer was pretty solitary most days. My family was off at work and school outside the house, my friends were scattered around town, and my anxiety was often too big to reach out for coffee or dinner dates.

I paused and took a breath. Looking at the computer screen in front of me, I took in the view of each little square as the face of a woman whose bravery and wisdom I adored stared back at me. Here was a grand opportunity. Here was a chance to put the years of therapy, of mindset shifts, of trust and bravery to the test in order to show myself that I was capable, strong, resilient, and free to become the next version of the woman I'd deeply known myself to be.

I scanned the monitor. I'd be able to finally meet all these beautiful faces in these tiny squares. I would be able to hug them beside an ocean view, to laugh and cry and break bread together. How glorious it would be to see their faces up close, to sense their presence, and to look directly into their eyes instead of a camera lens!

I wiped away my tears and picked up my phone to reply to the group text: "I'm in."

Once again, I had to lean into the belief that the benefits would outweigh the risks. I would have to trust that I'd find food I could eat, that I could show up fully as myself and not be ashamed of needing to do things differently when OCD or anxiety got in the way at any given moment. I had to keep showing up to my life, bravely carrying the fear along with me so that I could experience the joy and connection that saying yes to these opportunities would provide. These were the powerful steps, one resistant but willing yes at a time, that continued to allow me to grow, that would continue to make this life worth living.

I surrendered to that yes and began the preparations. I needed to have a sense of autonomy in the planning, and I chose a couple of trusted women I knew would help support me through the experience. I took charge of finding a place for us, creating shared documents with itineraries and such, and coordinated our arrival times and grocery needs.

I took the first leg of the trip solo—flying from Iowa to Denver, Colorado, where I got to meet my New Mexico bestie in the airport and fly the second leg with her into San Jose. I cried on takeoff; I clapped and cheered on landing. I arrived at the event as one of the few still wearing a mask in large groups. During the lunch break on the first day, I left to head back to the Airbnb I had carefully curated with a few ladies to keep exposures to a minimum and be able to have a kitchen to make my own food.

I'm not going to lie; the trip was hard: I barely slept, I got a migraine, I had nightmares, and I cried a lot. On day two, I had a panic attack on the way to the venue after lunch and had to stand in the back for much of the afternoon session, overwhelmed and spent. I snacked, and I avoided people, yet I continued to will myself to trust the process, to get back into the game after each break I took to regulate my nervous system.

However, there was also beauty and solace every time I returned to the present. Although the trip was challenging, I also laughed a lot. I got to walk on the beach with women I loved and truly cared for. I got to share moments of vulnerability, receiving and giving support in ways I'd never have been able to create long distance. I danced with my sisters; I stepped into more leadership and spoke on stage to hundreds of people; I unfurled my phoenix wings and flew higher, all on my own.

When it was time to travel home, I hugged my friends and cried for the joy and the loss. I'd miss sitting around the kitchen island with them, chatting about nothing and everything in a way that only proximity can lend itself. I wasn't quite ready to say goodbye, but I was also very ready to be home again.

On the final leg of the return trip, I was seated in a row with a man who looked to be in his thirties and totally uninterested in making any sort of small talk. That was okay by me, though sometimes chatting with others helps deflect the fear inside. I sat in the aisle seat, he was in the window seat, and the middle was vacant. The sun had just gone down before we boarded, and I was filled with a mix of exhaustion and readiness.

And I was starving. Home is really the only place I can eat without fear, and that isn't all the time either. I wanted to keep my stomach relatively empty for the flights, though; fear of getting motion sickness or having to get up and use the bathroom beat out any hunger pains, so I nibbled on the San Francisco Sourdough I'd picked up from an authentic bakery on a quick visit to the city with my cousin and dear friend before he dropped me off at the airport.

The plane took off, and I attempted to get the movie viewer in front of me started. The remote embedded in the armrest was broken. I had tried everything, so instead, I plugged my headphones into the armrest in the middle seat and watched a promo for some movie on repeat until the flight attendants started coming around with drinks and snacks. I let one of them know that the remote on my seat didn't work (just for future reference, if they ever wanted to fix it), and the man in the window seat perked up to offer some helpful advice.

"Yeah, it's all smashed in, so nothing is actually working," I noted after he told me which button did what. "I've actually been trying to watch this one," I pointed to the middle headrest, which was now playing sports news, "but I think I'm done trying." I then removed my headphones and looked out the window. "Are you from Iowa or just heading there to visit?" I asked him.

"I live there, heading home from a tech conference in Vegas," he responded.

I'd never been to Vegas and only knew its reputation. "Did you get any sleep?" I chuckled.

"Barely," he said. "We worked all day and partied pretty heavy most nights. I couldn't keep up, though. I was so ready to come home to my family the second day in."

We chatted a while longer. I learned that he had two young kids, and I offered some helpful hints about parenting during the toddler years. He let me in on a few new tech advances coming up, and we went a few rounds on the pros and cons of AI until we were interrupted by a voice on the loudspeaker.

"Ladies and gentleman, this is your captain speaking," said the voice. A little surge of adrenaline shot through my veins, but I redirected it with my breath and kept listening. "If you take a look out the left-hand side of the plane," the pilot continued, "you'll be able to get a glimpse of the aurora borealis. It's a pretty amazing sight."

I'd never seen the northern lights. When you live in Iowa, they rarely, if ever, come into view. I leaned in a bit to look out the window.

"Do you mind if I move to the middle seat for a minute to get a better look?" I asked. I felt mildly weird scooting closer to a stranger.

"Not at all," he replied. "In fact, I was going to run to the restroom. Go ahead and sit here for a minute." He gestured to his window seat, unbuckled, and scooted around me to head to the back of the plane.

I unhooked myself and slid over to the window, the bright green glow of the dancing lights now clearly in view.

I snapped a few pictures with my phone and sat still for a moment. So many things occurred to me at once. It felt as if the night sky was celebrating with me—the dancing lights that flickered along the edge of the Earth riding the waves of possibility.

We are not separate; the whole of everything in the universe connects us—the vibrations of sounds and atoms, the magnetism and mirrors. I rest in that deep knowing I have and am grateful when nature reminds me of that connection. When it feels so hard, when it feels hopeless and dark, there is a comfort in remembering that we are not alone, even when it feels so lonely.

This moment, and others like it, also allow me to understand that the fear I experience is a part of a deeper purpose I hold. It is the struggle I've known and also the catalyst that propels me to learn and grow. Again and again, I had to refuse to allow fear to hold me back and instead learn to appreciate what it was showing me, which is that I no longer have to fear the fear.

Instead, I can embrace fear and lean into its lessons and its opportunities. I can allow fear to be there and at the same time be open to a perspective of possibility and hope. I can do this by showing up authentically, by being more compassionate to myself and to others—especially when challenges surface. I can seek support and not feel ashamed to ask for help when needed.

There is a way through the darkness, and it starts with a willingness to believe another path is possible, even if we can't quite see it yet.

Every Day, I'm Brave is a way of life and a roadmap for how you too can show up bravely each and every day. We *can* create a life we love, no matter what diagnoses we've been handed. When anxiety, depression, OCD, or other challenges interfere with our everyday life or prevent us from working toward our goals and dreams, things can start to feel a little hopeless.

We have to decide for ourselves that it is worth the risk to try something different, to believe in our innate power to transform and elevate our lives, instead of continuing to allow fear to make all our decisions. We have to become conscious of our thoughts, feelings, and actions to become the best version of ourselves. We have to learn that thoughts are changeable, feelings are fluid, and putting too much weight on one or the other can leave us stuck, isolated, and ultimately profoundly sad. The more we can learn how to put our efforts toward purpose, passion, and people, the better we can become at creating a beautiful life—not in spite of the fear, but alongside it.

This book is a love letter to all of you who face similar challenges and sometimes feel like there's no way out. I see you. There is hope.

We can be brave, every day.

Brave Reflection

You are worthy. When you show up bravely every day, you give permission to others to do the same, and that allows us all to grow. My invitation to you here is to see a broader view: Maybe we are all just mirrors to one another. This human experience holds many collective, universal truths. Our stories can help us to understand, learn, and rise above the challenges we face, and we can learn from every experience so that we begin to make different choices from a more centered and conscious place. Judgment has no place here, only love. This, as it turns out, is a powerful perspective for healing.

In this final brave reflection, I invite you to get curious about how you can bring more love to the experience of fear. Use the following prompts to guide you:

- How can you love the parts of you that feel so afraid?

- What helps you remember that you're connected to nature, other people, and your place in this world even when it is hard to feel it?

- How can you allow fear the space it needs to exist and keep taking bold action toward your goals and dreams anyway so that you continue to show up bravely every day?

Share your wisdom on social media alongside #EveryDay-ImBrave to send more love out into the world. Then, head over to www.everydayimbrave.com to learn more and connect with others on the path. Together, we are brave. Every. Single. Day.

ACKNOWLEDGMENTS

THIS BOOK HAS BEEN A REFLECTION of life in process, and I have so many people to thank for getting this project out of my head and into your hands.

To Jena Schwartz, my first writing coach: You not only inspired me to start a blog nearly fifteen years ago but also gave me the tools, accountability, and confidence to boldly share my story in its pieces over the years. You were the first person I called when I was ready to get serious about the book, and you helped me launch into a committed practice and pursuit of the narrative arc that would become *Every Day, I'm Brave*.

To Maggie Langrick, CEO and chief editor of Wonderwell Press, who read my proposal and the ragged draft of this book and became an immediate champion of its message: Thank you for believing in me and opening the door to possibility even wider.

To Amanda Hoppe, my developmental editor, who understood (even when I didn't) how this story should best be put together: Thank you for your wisdom, your inquiry, the nudging, and the deadlines. You helped make clear the lessons that were woven and embedded in the moments I had chosen to reveal, and you helped me stay devoted to the path of writing and rewriting until this mosaic revealed a consistent message of acceptance, hope, bravery, and transformation. Your guidance was a salve in this process.

To my editing and publishing team at Greenleaf Publishing, without whom this book would just be a printed PDF in a folder on my desk: I'm grateful for the expertise, guidance, deadlines, and amplification of this message from each person who helped along the way.

To Maria Heart Song, my energetic support from across the ocean: You helped me stay true to my heart, my message, my body, and my soul's mission as the reality of this book took shape and the energy of the launch got scary. Your work provides safety and comfort and continues to empower me to stay grounded while reaching for the stars. You are the power grid behind so many lighthouses across the globe. Thank you for your bravery that shows others the way.

To Sage Lavine and my Women Rocking Business colleagues, coaches, sisters, and dear friends: Thank you for seeing me and showing me another way through. I love you all so very much.

To the beautiful women in my Writer's Room who continue to inspire me: I created the space to get serious about writing, and when others showed up, I was honored. We make magic together. Thank you for committing to your own writing practice so that your messages can create a ripple effect of good in the world.

To Ama (Amandine) Mothershed, my dear friend and executive assistant, who helped me manage many tasks of my business and kept the ball rolling as we leveled up. I'm so grateful for your friendship, guidance, and support.

To Bev, whose willingness to read and reflect on the rough drafts of this book over coffee dates was a pure gift: Your own story is a powerful one, and I am excited for its wings to unfurl.

To Dave: You didn't let me forget that exercise is a form of self-love and just as important to my mental well-being.

To M, whose strength and resilience inspire me to stand taller and work harder to put this message out there: Your heart is big and bold, and I will forever be in your corner.

To my therapists past and present: I've learned so much from each of you at every evolution, and I thank you for helping me become who I am today.

To my family of origin, my brothers, their daughters, and all of our extended family, especially the amazing women who came before me, including my grandmothers and aunts (especially Auntie Judy) who bravely paved the way for the working woman, juggling marriage and family and purpose work: You have shaped me in ways that will continue to be revealed.

To my parents, Jane and Stanley: I am grateful for your love, guidance, acceptance, and support—even when you weren't quite sure what I was up to. Thank you for believing in me anyway and for all the ways you show up for us. I love you both so much.

To my bonus children, Bella and Tobey, and their mom, Jennifer: I'm so grateful for the modern family we continue to be. Your hearts mean the world to me.

To Benjamin: You uplift me in ways that propel me forward, your wisdom and expertise help me (even if I'm slow to admit it sometimes), and I honor all the ways in which you hold the hearts of the many people you serve, including all of us at home. Thank you for the gifts of your children, Sarah and Noah, who bring joy, laughter, and light. I am grateful for the grounding force of our connection that allows me to take action toward my dreams. I love you very much.

To my children, Shelby, Evan, and Lily: You continue to be my greatest teachers. May you always show up bravely in your own lives, even when it may feel impossible to do so. You are brilliant and strong in myriad, mysterious, and beautifully diverse ways. I love you, forever and always.

ABOUT THE AUTHOR

RENEE ZUKIN IS AN AUTHOR AND MENTOR with more than twenty years of experience in education, writing, and entrepreneurship combined. In addition, she has spent decades studying multiple psychological and healing modalities that have sustained her and helped support her students and clients alike. She is passionate about cultivating a safe space for others to use the written word as a tool for self-transformation and empowerment.

Renee earned her bachelor of arts in language and literature from the University of Michigan and her master of arts in teaching from the University of Iowa. In addition, she has studied mindfulness for educators, restorative justice, and community circles. She is a lifelong learner of personal growth and a passionate proponent of living consciously.

Learn more at: www.reneezukin.com.